VIKRAMORVASI,

AN INDIAN DRAMA

VIKRAMORVASI,

AN INDIAN DRAMA;

TRANSLATED INTO ENGLISH PROSE FROM THE SANSKRIT
OF KALIDASA,

BY

EDWARD BYLES COWELL,

OF MAGDALEN HALL, OXFORD.

GYAN

Published by

GYAN

Gyan Publishing House
5, Ansari Road
Daryaganj, New Delhi-110002
Phone: 011-47034999, 9811692060
E-mail: books@gyanbooks.com

Distribution Network
gyanbooks.com
India, USA, Canada, UK, Australia, France

ISBN: 978-81-212-7330-5 (PB)
First Published, 1851

2nd Impression 2023

Printed at: Gyan Press, Delhi.

VIKRAMORVASI, AN INDIAN DRAMA
Translator: EDWARD BYLES COWELL

VIKRAMORVAŚÍ,

AN INDIAN DRAMA;

TRANSLATED INTO ENGLISH PROSE FROM THE SANSKRIT
OF KÁLIDÁSA,

BY

EDWARD BYLES COWELL,

OF MAGDALEN HALL, OXFORD.

HERTFORD:
PRINTED AND PUBLISHED BY STEPHEN AUSTIN,
BOOKSELLER TO THE EAST-INDIA COLLEGE.

MDCCCLI.

"I revere the rhythm as well as the rhyme, by which poetry first becomes poetry; but that which is really, deeply, and fundamentally effective, that which is really permanent and furthering, is that which remains of the poet when he is translated into *prose*. Then remains the pure, perfect substance; of which, when absent, a dazzling exterior often contrives to make a false show; and which, when present, such an exterior contrives to conceal."

GOETHE *(Auto-biography.)*

PREFACE.

THE following translation has been undertaken to supply the Sanskrit student with a literal version of a highly esteemed work, which has been lately made a text-book by Mr. MONIER WILLIAMS' edition. The first object, therefore, of the translator has been to give his author's literal meaning; elegance of style has been throughout esteemed secondary, although he has endeavoured, as far as he was able, to combine the two. He refers his readers to Professor WILSON'S *Specimens of the Theatre of the Hindús*, for a fine scholarly translation in verse: the following pages aspire to be only a faithful transcript of the original in prose.

Vikramorvas'í is a drama by the same elegant hand that wrote *Śakúntalá* (which was translated in prose by Sir W. JONES at the close of the last century)—tradition and internal evidence alike bearing witness to the identity of authorship. In each we see the same exquisite polish of style, the same light touch in painting scenery and character; and yet the two dramas are 'like in difference,' and each has the separate personality, as well as the mutual likeness, which characterises the twin offspring of the same creating mind.* KÁLIDÁSA is believed to have flourished during the century which preceded our era, and tradition names him as one of the "nine gems" of the court of Vikramáditya.

The translator would forbear to make any remarks on the drama, with the exception of the Fourth Act, which requires a few words of introduction. In the Sanskrit dramas, the heroes alone talk Sanskrit, the women and inferior characters speak in Prákrit, a dialect derived from Sanskrit by a similar series of changes to those which have melted Latin into the modern Italian and Spanish. Now, through the greater part of this act, KÁLIDÁSA

* Both dramas are founded on ancient legends. A few meagre hints in the "*Mahábhárata*" (vol. i., p. 113), appear to have furnished the first idea of the amplified story of the "*Vikramorvas'í*." The Pauránic version appears in the *Harivans'a*.

makes his hero use Prákrit instead of Sanskrit; and this artistic change of dialect shews that he felt that Pururavas was, in this act, departing from the *víra rasa* or ideal of heroism. He is mad, but his madness is not that of "Orestes" or "Lear," for we are in the world of the soft contemplative Hindú; and wherever we turn in Indian poetry, we find the gentler feelings of the heart, but not the fiercer. The reader must bear this in mind as he follows Pururavas through the forest, and forget for the while Orestes' frenzied call for his bow, or Lear's desolation in the storm.

I have followed Mr. Williams' text; but have also consulted Lenz, and especially his "*Apparatus Criticus*" (published in 1834), which contains some useful *scholia* from a MS. in the East India House Library; Professor Wilson's translation has also frequently afforded me much assistance.

I may add that, in the numerous stage-directions, I have not always kept the word *nátya* 'gesticulation.' It is probable that the Hindu stage was nearly destitute of all accessories to the performance, these being left to the imagination of the spectator; motion in a chariot, etc., were thus merely represented by gesticulation; but

I have not thought it necessary to preserve this very prosaic feature in the translation. I have also followed Professor WILSON in his rendering of the title of the Drama; on the Continent, other interpretations have been suggested, as "*Urvasiæ Incessus*," etc.; the last German Translation, by HÖFER, gives it as "*Urwas'í der Preis der Tapferkeit*," which agrees with LENZ' last suggestion, in his "*Apparatus*" p. 9. *Vikramapráptorvasí*. I have also adopted LENZ's and BOEHTLINGK's interpretation of the words *Praves'aka* and *Vishkambhaka*.

EXPLANATION OF SOME TERMS OF MYTHOLOGY, ETC.

Ananga, a name of Káma.

Bharata, the name of a sage, the dramatic instructor of the Nymphs.

Chátaka, a bird, supposed to live only on rain.

Chowrie, the white bushy tail of the Thibet cow, which serves for a flapper, and is also used as an ornament for horses, like the plume of the war-horse of chivalry.

Dánava, Daitya, or Asura, a kind of Titan or demon.

Durgá or Párvatí, the wife of Siva.

Gandharva, a celestial musician.

Garuda, the King of Birds.

Indra, the god of the visible firmament.

Kalpa, the name of a tree in Indra's paradise.

Káma, the god of love.

Kartikeya, the god of war.

Kuvera, the god of wealth.

Lakshmí, the wife of Vishnu.

Márisha, a title given to the principal actor.

Nandana or Swarga, Indra's paradise.

Sachi or Paulomí, the wife of Indra.

Saraswatí, the wife of Bráhma, and goddess of eloquence.

KÁLIDÁSA'S

VIKRAMORVAŚÍ.

PROLOGUE.

BENEDICTION.

May He, whom they call the Sole Male in the Vedántas, pervading heaven and earth, to whom alone, in its full meaning, belongs the title of "Lord," who is sought within by those who desire liberation, with suspended breath and other penances—Śiva, who is ever ready to be found, by firm faith and meditation,—be your final beatitude!

MANAGER.

[*After the benediction is ended.*

Enough of this prolixity. (*Looking towards the actors' room.*) *Márisha!* this assembly hath seen the sentimental compositions of former poets; I am now about to appear before it with a new play, strung together by the art of Kálidása, entitled "Vikramorvaśí;" do thou, then, command our company, that every actor be attentive to his part.

Enter an ACTOR.

ACTOR.

Sir, your commands shall be fulfilled.

MANAGER.

I would meanwhile, with bowed head, address the reverend and learned in this assembly. I beseech you all, by your kindness to your friends, or at least by your admiration of a good drama, hear with attention the present work of Kálidása.

[*A Voice is heard behind the scenes.*

Help, ye noble! help!

MANAGER.

Ha! why is heard this sudden cry of distress from the beings who ride in their aërial chariots through the sky? (*Having thought a moment.*) Ah! I have it! It is the heavenly nymph, who was born from the thigh of the Muni, the friend of Nara;* who, returning from visiting the Lord of Kailása, has been seized in mid-journey by the demon-foes of the gods, and therefore does yonder troop of nymphs shriek for succour.

[*Exeunt.*

* Indra sent some nymphs to tempt Náráyana while engaged in penance; the sage, to shame them, took up a flower and placed it on his thigh; and it immediately became a beautiful nymph, hence named Urvas'i.

ACT I.

Enter some NYMPHS, *hurriedly.*

NYMPHS.

Help, ye noble! help! whosoever is the friend of the immortals, or hath his way in the sky.

Enter, hurriedly, a KING *in his chariot, with his* CHARIOTEER.

KING.

Cease your cries, approach and tell me, Pururavas, now returning from the Sun,—against what are ye to be helped?

RAMBHÁ.

Against the insolence of the demons.

KING.

What wrong has been done you by their insolence?

RAMBHÁ.

Let the great King hear! She, who was Indra's soft weapon, when he was alarmed at the greatness of a Sage's penance;—the shamer of Párvatí, proud of her beauty; and the ornament of heaven; she, our loved companion, returning from the palace of Kuvera, has been carried off midway, with Chitralekhá, by a Dánava.

KING.

Is it known towards what quarter the miscreant is gone?

NYMPHS.

Towards the north-east.

Vasantasená is called *praharanam anangasya.*—MRICH., p. 163.

KING.

Dismiss your sorrows; I will strive to bring back your friend.

NYMPHS.

[*Joyfully.*

Well worthy is the action of a descendant of the Lunar race!

KING.

Where will ye, meantime, await my return?

NYMPHS.

On yonder peak of Hemakuta.

KING.

Charioteer! urge the horses to their utmost speed towards the north-eastern quarter.

CHARIOTEER.

As the King commands.

KING.

[*Gesticulating the swift motion of the chariot.*

Excellent! Excellent! with such a speed as this, I could overtake even Garuda, though he had the start! Before my chariot rise the clouds in flakes, as rises the dust; the swift rolling of the wheels seems to create a second range of spokes between the first; the long chowrie on the head of the steed stands motionless as in a picture; and the banner in the middle streams to the end of the car, from the wind of our speed.

[*Exeunt.*

SAHAJANYÁ.

Dear friend, the King is gone; let us, too, set forth to the spot as appointed.

MENAKÁ.

Dearest, let us do so.

[*They climb the peak of Hemakuta.*

RAMBHÁ.

Will the King, indeed, succeed in extracting this barb of anguish from our hearts?

MENAKÁ.

Doubt not, dear friend.

RAMBHÁ.

Surely the Dánavas are hard to be conquered.

MENAKÁ.

Even great Indra himself, as the hour of battle draws near, summons this most honoured hero from the earth, and posts him in the van of his army, to win victory for the gods.

RAMBHÁ.

May he be altogether victorious!

MENAKÁ.

[*Standing still for a moment.*

Dear friends! take heart, and be of good cheer; yonder I see the chariot which the Moon gave to the holy King, gleaming with the banner that bears the ensign of the deer, and I divine that he will not come unsuccessful back.

[*They gesticulate as at some sign, and stand looking. Then enter the* KING *and his* CHARIOTEER, *in the aërial chariot, with* URVASÍ, *whose eyes are closed in terror, leaning on the right hand of* CHITRALEKHÁ.

CHITRALEKHÁ.

Dearest! revive! revive!

KING.

Fairest maiden! revive! revive! thy terrors from the demon are dispelled, O timid one! the majesty of the Thunderer guards the three worlds: open therefore, I pray, those long eyes of thine, as the lotus-lake its lotuses at the end of the night.

CHITRALEKHÁ.

It is strange; not even yet has she regained her consciousness; and, but for her breathing, there is no symptom of life.

KING.

Greatly, indeed, was thy poor friend alarmed; the heavy beating of her heart betrays itself by that wreath of Mandára blossoms, and she sighs repeatedly between her full breasts.

CHITRALEKHÁ.

[*In a mournful voice.*

Dearest Urvas'í! I beseech thee, recover thyself; one might have deemed that thou wast no nymph of heaven at all!

KING.

The tremor of fear hath not yet forsaken her heart, tender like a flower; but it is still told by yonder edge of her robe, as it rises and falls with the sighing of her bosom.

[URVAŚÍ *comes to herself.*

KING.

[*Joyfully.*

Joy to thee, O Chitralekhá! thy dear friend hath regained her consciousness; see, like the night, when it escapes from darkness, at the rising of the Moon; or like the flame of the nocturnal fire, when it bursts through the thickness of the smoke, thy fair-formed companion is seen freed from her fainting; like Gangá, as she flows back into serenity, when the fall of a bank hath troubled her waters.

CHITRALEKHÁ.

Dear Urvas'í! lay aside your fear,—they have been conquered by a Monarch who compassionates the distressed;—the Dánavas, the enemies of the gods, have had their hopes all smitten down.*

URVAŚÍ.

[*Opening her eyes.*

What? did great Indra behold the fray, and come to my rescue?

CHITRALEKHÁ.

Not Indra, but this holy king, Pururavas, himself a very Indra in majesty.

* "*Sakhi, Urvas'í, vis'wastá bhava, ápannánukampiná mahárájena paráhatáh khalu te; tridas'aparipanthino hatás'á Dánaváh.*" I should prefer the absence of the semicolon, in which case *hatás'á* would simply mean "cruel," and *te* would be construed with *Dánaváh.*

URVAŚÍ.

[*Aside, looking at the* KING.

What a kindness hath my fright from the Dánava proved!

KING.

[*Aside, looking at* URVAŚÍ.

Well might all the nymphs, as they tempted the holy Náráyana in his devotions, stand silent with shame, when they beheld her, as she sprang from his thigh; or rather, I feel sure that she was no creation of the ascetic at all. Say, was it the Moon, the giver of brightness, who called her into being? or Káma himself, his whole soul immersed in love? or was it the month that is richest with flowers? How, indeed, could an aged Sage, cold with continued study of the Vedas, and his desires turned away from all objects of sense, create this heart-bewitching form?

URVAŚÍ.

Dear Chitralekhá, where can our friends be?

CHITRALEKHÁ.

The mighty monarch knows, who hath delivered us from our fears.

KING.

[*Looking at* URVAŚÍ.

Thy friends are in the deepest distress; for only consider,—even *he*, before whose happy eyes thou hast but once tarried of thine own accord, even *he*, fair lady, without thee will be mournful with longing; how, then, must thy friends fare when parted from thee, whose love hath grown up with their growth?

URVASÍ.

[*To herself.*

Thy words are very ambrosia; but what marvel that *ambrosia* should come from the *Moon?** (*Aloud, to the* KING): Hence is it that my heart so hastens after them.

KING.

[*Pointing with his hand.*

Yonder, fair lady, thy companions stand on Hemakúta, and look on thy face, gazing with longing eyes, as on the Moon escaped from Ráhu.

[URVASÍ *looks with longing.*

CHITRALEKHÁ.

Dearest, why dost thou look at me thus?

URVASÍ.

My eyes drink in that sharer of my joys and sorrows——

CHITRALEKHÁ.

[*Smiling.*

Whom meanest thou?

URVASÍ.

[*Recovering herself.*

Whom should I mean but yonder troop of my friends?

RAMBHÁ.

[*Looking joyously.*

Dearest! see! the holy King approaches, bringing back our loved Urvas'í, with Chitralekhá; like the Moon, attended by its asterism Vis'ákhá.

* Pururavas is of the lunar race, and the Moon is the reservoir of ambrosia (*amrita*).

MENAKÁ.

[*Looking.*

Dearest! two delightful things have now happened to us, for our companion is restored to us, and the holy King himself is unhurt.

SAHAJANYÁ.

It was *you* who said, "The Dánava is hard to be conquered."

KING.

Charioteer! make the car descend on yonder mountain-peak.

CHARIOTEER.

As the King (long may he live!)* commands.

[*He does so;* URVASÍ *is shaken by the motion, and leans timidly upon the* KING.

KING.

[*Aside.*

Ah! our descent to earth bears a happy fruit! My body, from the shaking of the chariot, has felt the touch of this long-eyed maiden's side, and every hair seems to shoot forth with love.

URVASÍ.

[*Ashamed, to* CHITRALEKHÁ.

Remove a little further.

CHITRALEKHÁ.

I cannot: indeed I cannot.

* *A'yushmat* is properly used as an honorary title; I have translated it at length in the present instance, to explain its meaning. The *Sáhitya-darpana* gives it as the proper mode of address from a charioteer to a warrior.

RAMBHÁ.

Let us go to meet the gracious monarch!

ALL THE NYMPHS.

Let us do so! [*They approach.*

KING.

Charioteer! stay the car, while this fair-browed maiden, herself desiring, steps forth to join her desiring friends; as the Beauty of the Spring, the creepers!

[*The* CHARIOTEER, *complying, stops the chariot.*

THE NYMPHS.

Hail! may the King be ever victorious!

KING.

And you, too, may ye be happy in your companion's return!

URVASÍ.

[*Having alighted, leaning upon* CHITRALEKHÁ's *hand.*

Dear friends! give me a close embrace; I had not a hope in my heart, that I should ever see my loved companions again.

[*Her friends embrace her.*

MENAKÁ.

[*In a tone of prayer.*

May the great King ever guard the whole earth!

CHARIOTEER.

O King! a great host of chariots has suddenly burst into view; and yonder comes some one, who, decked with bracelets of molten gold, alights from the sky, and ascends the mountain-peak, like a lightning cloud!

THE NYMPHS.

Oh! wonderful! Behold Chitraratha!

Enter CHITRARATHA.

CHITRARATHA.

[*Advancing to the* KING.

Hail! Success to the heroic valour which is able to render such assistance.

KING.

Ah! the King of the Gandharvas! (*He alights from the car*). Welcome to my dear friend!

[*They grasp each other's hand.*

CHITRARATHA.

Oh my friend! as soon as Indra heard that Urvas'í was carried off by the demon Kes'i, he bade the Gandharva hosts haste to her rescue; but having heard immediately afterwards, from the heavenly spirits,* of the weight of glory that thou hast won, I am come forthwith to thee here; wilt thou, then, take charge of the maiden, and come to behold great Indra himself? Thou hast, indeed, achieved a mighty action, and one dear to his heart. She whom once Náráyana gave to the wind-god, has been won by thee, his friend, from the Daitya's hand, and regiven to him as a new gift to-day!

KING.

O friend! speak not so! The heroism is all Indra's

* Literally, "the riders in *vimáná*, or heavenly chariots."

own, if his friends overcome his foes; the very echo of the lion's roar strikes the elephants with terror, as it rolls forth from the mountain glens.

CHITRARATHA.

It is well! Modesty is the ornament of valour.

KING.

My friend! this is not a time for me to see Indra: do thou, therefore, thyself conduct yonder lady to the presence of our lord.

CHITRARATHA.

It shall be as thou wilt. Ladies! let us depart.

[*They all set out.*

URVASÍ.

[*To her friend.*

Dear Chitralekhá! I cannot say farewell to the great king, who hath saved us; do thou, therefore, be my voice.*

CHITRALEKHÁ.

[*Approaching the* KING.

O mighty monarch! Urvasí sends thee this message: "I desire," she says, "to take my leave of the king, and with me to carry his fame, as a friend, to the world of the immortals."

KING.

May we part to meet again!

[*The* NYMPHS *all set forth through the air, with the* GANDHARVA.

* *Literally,* "my mouth."

URVAŚÍ.

[*Pretending to be stopped in her flight.*

How strange! my garland is caught and entwined by the branch of this creeping plant. (*Turning and casting a stolen glance at the* KING.) Oh! dearest Chitralekhá! I beseech thee, release it.

CHITRALEKHÁ.

[*Looking and smiling.*

Ah! it is, indeed, firmly held. I cannot release it.

URVAŚÍ.

A truce to laughing! pray unloose it.

CHITRALEKHÁ.

It seems to me very fast, but still I will unloose it.

URVAŚÍ.

[*Forcing a smile.*

Dearest! you will remember your words.

KING.

It was a kind action of thine, O creeper! in my behalf—to interpose this momentary obstacle in her path; since once again have I seen this maiden with the arched eye, her face half-turned towards me.

[CHITRALEKHÁ *releases her.* URVAŚÍ, *after looking back to the* KING, *beholds, with a sigh, her companions in their upward flight.*

CHARIOTEER.

Behold, O King! having hurled the Daityas, the guilty rebels against Indra, deep down into the briny ocean, thy aerial weapon hath returned into its quiver, like a great snake to its den.

KING.

Do thou, therefore, stay the chariot, while I ascend.

[*The* KING *ascends.*

URVAŚÍ.

[*Looking with a fond glance towards the* KING.

Shall I—shall I ever see that deliverer again?

[*Exit with the* GANDHARVA *and her companions.*

KING.

[*Gazing upwards after her.*

Alas! that love should always desire the unattainable! This heavenly maiden, as she flies upward to the central home of her father, irresistibly draws after her the soul from my body, as the flamingo draws the filament from the blossom-shorn lotus-stalk.

END OF THE FIRST ACT.

ACT II.

Enter the GRACIOSO.

GRACIOSO.

[*Flurriedly.*

Away, O inviter! In this concourse of people I cannot restrain my tongue, with this secret of the king's swelling in my mouth like an oblation of boiled rice. While, therefore, the King is gone to the judgment-seat, I will go up to yonder temple, away from the press of the throng, and wait there. (*He walks round, and sits down, covering his mouth with his hands.*)

Enter a FEMALE SERVANT.

FEMALE SERVANT.

This is the command which I have received from my lady the daughter of the King of Kás'í, "My faithful Nipuniká," she said, "ever since the King returned from visiting the Sun, he has seemed as if he had left his heart behind him; do thou, therefore, try and learn from the venerable Mánavaka the real cause of his sadness." Now, in what way should I put the question to the Bráhman? I will venture a guess that the King's secret, like the hoar-frost on a blade of grass, will not long stay with him; I will therefore, forthwith, go and seek him. (*She walks round and sees him.*) But, strange to say! there, I declare

Mánavaka is standing, hiding himself in yonder corner, like an ape in a picture, and deep in thought on something or other. I will go up to him. (*She approaches.*) I salute thee, reverend Sir!

GRACIOSO.

I return thy greeting. (*Aside.*) The moment that I look on this odious maid, the King's secret begins bursting my heart, and well nigh forces its way out! (*Aloud, partly covering his mouth*) Oh, Nipuniká! whither art thou going? thus leaving thy music-practice.

SERVANT.

To visit your reverend self, on an especial commission from the Queen.

GRACIOSO.

What may be her Highness's commands?

SERVANT.

"O reverend Bráhman!" she says, "there is a great lack of kindness in thy conduct towards me; thou regardest me not in my present anxiety."

GRACIOSO.

Oh, Nipuniká! has any offence been committed by my my beloved friend?

SERVANT.

You know the woman for whom he sorrows; he has actually addressed the Queen by *her* name.

GRACIOSO.

[*To himself.*

What! my friend, then, has himself revealed the secret! How then can a Bráhman like me hold his tongue any longer? (*Aloud.*) Ah! you mean the noble nymph Urvas'í; since he became mad from the sight of her, the Queen is not the only person whom he hath distressed,—*me* too, a Bráhman, he hath most grievously afflicted by rigorously keeping me away from all food!

SERVANT.

[*Aside.*

I have attained my end, and broken open my Lord's impregnable secret; I will go at once and tell it to her Highness. (*She begins to retire.*)

GRACIOSO.

Oh Nipuniká! I beseech thee bear this message of mine to the daughter of the King of Kás'i; tell her, "I am utterly wearied with endeavouring to turn my loved friend, from following this deceitful mirage; but if he can only behold your highness's lotus face, I am sure he will be effectually won back."

SERVANT.

As you command, sir.

[*Exit.*

The Bard proclaims behind the scenes:—

May the King be ever victorious! dispelling to the ends of the earth all darkness from thy people;—the energy of thy power and that of the sun's, seem alike in our eyes. The Lord of the stars stands alone for a moment in the midst of the sky; and thou, too, O King! takest thy rest in this sixth portion of the day!

GRACIOSO.

[*Listening.*

My loved friend has risen from the judgment-seat; and in very truth here he comes; I will, therefore, attend at his side.

[*Exit.*

(END OF THE PRAVEŚAKA.)

Enter the KING, *oppressed with melancholy, followed by the* GRACIOSO.

KING.

That beauty of the world of the Immortals hath entered at first sight into my heart, the way being opened by the irresistible arrow of Káma.

GRACIOSO.

Yes! and the daughter of the King of Káśí seems, in truth, to take it much to heart.

KING.

[*Looking fixedly at him.*

Will you tell me how the secret got abroad?

GRACIOSO.

[*Aside.*

I have been tricked by that daughter of a slave, Nipuniká; otherwise, why should my friend ask this question?

KING.

Why do you stand thus silent?

GRACIOSO.

Verily my tongue was tied so fast that I could not even make it answer the King.

KING.

It is well;—with what shall I now try to divert myself?

GRACIOSO.

Oh! let us go into the kitchen.

KING.

And what shall we do there?

GRACIOSO.

Let the enjoyment of the five kinds of viands, with the choicest delicacies, gladden your melancholy with sweetmeats, candied sugar, and cakes.

KING.

You, indeed, will be happy there with the various forms of your favourite dishes; but how should I be gladdened, who only seek the unattainable?

GRACIOSO.

You have crossed, I tell you, the path of the lady Urvaśí's vision.

KING.

What then?

GRACIOSO.

I expect that you will not find her so very unattainable.

KING.

The equal of her beauty must needs be superhuman.

GRACIOSO.

You rouse my curiosity! What matters the lady Urvaśí's beauty? I am sure I am considered second after her!

KING.

I have never yet described her limb by limb; hear it in a few words.

GRACIOSO.

I am all attention.

KING.

Oh! my friend! her form is the ornament of ornaments; itself adds the grace to all lovely decorations, and it mocks the similitude of all comparisons.

GRACIOSO.

Well! well! you embrace this exquisite beauty in your quicksilver-chase, only as the thirsty Chátaka follows the mirage.

KING.

Oh! my friend! cool retreats* are the only refuge for my fevered soul;—lead the way at once to the pleasure-garden.

GRACIOSO.

What's to be done?—This is the way; lo! here is the pleasure-garden's enclosure. (*They walk round*). See, too, without waiting for your command, the south wind has hastened hither to welcome you.†

KING.

Well-suited, indeed, is the character of the breeze. Lo! here it comes, dropping on its way the beauty of the Spring, and making the twining jasmine play; it seems to me like a lover, from the union of affection and kindness.

GRACIOSO.

May it be like *you* in constancy! Will your highness enter the garden?

* *Literally*, "cold appliances."

† I have here followed the reading भवं (prakrit for भवान्) instead of भवेत्, which Lenz found in all the MSS. See his *Apparatus Criticus*, p. 12.

KING.

Enter thou first, my friend.

[*They enter.*

KING.

[*Trembling.*

Alas! my friend! I thought that I should heal my melancholy, if I strolled into the garden; but far otherwise is it proved by the event. This fair enclosure, after all, yields no rest, though I longed to enter it; like the great wave that stops the traveller's swimming, while he is carried away by the stream.*

GRACIOSO.

How so?

KING.

The god with the five arrows had even before this too deeply wounded my heart, and in vain I strove to repress its fond desires after the unattainable; but how much deeper now is the wound, when I see the young branches put forth by the Mangoes whose pale leaves are torn by the wind that blows fresh from Malaya?

GRACIOSO.

Let your highness cease these complaints; ere long the god of love will be your friend, and will guide you to the attainment of your desires.

KING.

I accept the good omen from the Bráhman's lips.

[*They walk round.*

* The Scholiast (LENZ *App. Crit.*) explains *pratípataranam*, by *pratikulaplavanam*.

GRACIOSO.

Only look, I beseech you, at the beauty of the garden, with the *Avatár* of spring revealed.

KING.

I am looking at it at every step. Lo! yonder, in front of us, is the Kuruvaka-blossom, pink like a woman's nails, and dark at either edge; and there the young As'oka-blossom, looking up as it opens, ever ready to be won by proffered caresses. And yonder hangs the fresh branch of the Amra tree, with its sprays brown with the yet scanty pollen of its flowers; O! my friend! how the Spring stands between Beauty and Youth as its companions!

GRACIOSO.

See! this bower of Mádhavi creepers, with its seat of black stone, and its blossoms all covered with swarms of bees, seems made of its own accord for your service; let it receive your favour.

KING.

As you please.

[*They sit down.*

GRACIOSO.

Here, then seated on such a seat, O King! let your eyes seek the lovely creeping plants, and smile away your desires after Urvas'í.

KING.

[*Sighing deeply.*

O! my friend! even in yon creepers of the garden, with their lovely branches and all their profusion of blossoms, the eye cannot find its rest, which languishes from the sight of that maiden! O! think of some remedy for *this!*

GRACIOSO.

[*Considering.*

Well! I am thinking; but do not again, I pray you, break the thread of my thoughts by your complainings. (*Making a sudden motion to himself*). Ah! I see what is to be done!

KING.

That maiden with a face bright like the full moon, is, alas! far beyond my reach;—what, then, means this sudden portent, which Káma works within me? My heart in a moment hath attained serenity, as though the bliss, which it sighs for, were really present before it.

[*He sits lost in a love reverie.*

At this moment enter, aloft in the air, URVASÍ *and* CHITRALEKHÁ.

CHITRALEKHÁ.

Dear Urvas'í! whither are you going, without mentioning the reason of your journey?

URVASÍ.

[*With an expression of love-sorrow, mingled with shame.*

Dear friend! when I said to you, on the peak of Hemakúta, "O! release my garland, which is entanged in the branch of a creeper," you smiled as you answered, "It is, indeed, firmly held, and it cannot be unloosed!" and do you ask me *now* whither I am going without mentioning the reason of my journey?

CHITRALEKHÁ.

Are you then, indeed, set out to visit the holy king, Pururavas?

URVAŚÍ.

This is, indeed, my purpose,—disregarding all the misgivings of shame.

CHITRALEKHÁ.

But whom has my dear Urvas'í sent before her.

URVAŚÍ.

Whom, indeed—but my heart?

CHITRALEKHÁ.

Yet even now, pause awhile and consider.

URVAŚÍ.

Love truly orders me forward,—how can I then stay to consider?

CHITRALEKHÁ.

Then I can say nothing more.

URVAŚÍ.

Dear friend! pray then shew me the path, by which I shall meet no hindrance in my going thither.

CHITRALEKHÁ.

Be of good cheer;—the holy preceptor of the Gods has taught us the spell called *Invincible*, of "binding the braid." With this we are rendered safe from any of the enemies of the Gods.

URVAŚÍ.

All this my heart knows well, and yet still I stand irresolute in my excessive fear.

[*Both fly onwards.*

CHITRALEKHÁ.

Look, dear Urvaśí! look here!—we are come to the Palace of the holy King, which rises like a crest over the city Pratishtháṇa, as it stands viewing its reflected image in the pure waters of Gangá, at their meeting with Yamuná.

URVAŚÍ.

[*With longing looks.*

Oh! it may be truly said that heaven itself seems to have entered this spot. Oh! my friend, where is that compassionator of the distressed?

CHITRALEKHÁ.

We shall know if we alight in this fair garden, which seems like some glade of the groves of Nandana.

[*They both descend.*

CHITRALEKHÁ.

Lo! yonder, dearest, he stands awaiting thee, like the newly-risen Moon, the Moonlight.*

* This *distinctive* personification of the Moon and its light is not unfrequent. Thus (Gorresio's Rámáyana, vol. iii., p. 273) Ráma says "that his wife Śítá had left him as the splendour leaves the Sun, when it sinks in the West."

URVAŚÍ.

Oh, my friend! the great King seems still dearer to look upon than even when first I saw him.

CHITRALEKHÁ.

It should be so,—come, then, let us approach him.

URVAŚÍ.

I will not approach him yet. I will first conceal myself in my veil,* and stand by his side, and listen to what he is deliberating upon with his bosom friend, in this solitary place.

CHITRALEKHÁ.

As you please.

[*They do so.*

GRACIOSO.

[*To the* KING.

Oh! at last I have discovered a plan for thy meeting with this object of thy love, though she be so hard to be won.

URVAŚÍ.

[*To* CHITRALEKHÁ.

Alas! who may this happy woman be, who knows the joy to be wooed by *him*?

CHITRALEKHÁ.

Why do you hesitate to discover the secret by your divine faculty of Meditation?

URVAŚÍ.

Alas! I fear to know it too quickly by my power.

* *Velo, quo me invisibilem reddo*—LENZ.

GRACIOSO.

[*To the* KING.

Yes, I repeat it. I have discovered a plan for thy meeting with this difficult object.

KING.

Speak it forth, my friend.

GRACIOSO.

Let your highness be an assiduous votary of Sleep, for it is Sleep who brings lovers together in its dreams: or paint an image of the lady Urvas'í in a picture, and solace thy heart to its fill with gazing on it.

URVAŚÍ.

[*Aside.*

Beat freely again, O my heart!

KING.

Both your plans are alike failures; only look,—this heart of mine is pierced through with the arrows of Káma; how then can I find that sleep which would bring me her presence in its dreams? Nor even if I obtained in a picture my beloved of the beautiful countenance, would the tear-floods stop, O my friend! which *will* rise in my eyes.

CHITRALEKHÁ.

[*To* URVAŚÍ.

Dearest! do you hear these words?

URVAŚÍ.

I hear them, but they are still not enough for my heart.

GRACIOSO.

[*To the* KING.

Well; no further reaches my ingenuity!

KING.

[*Sighing.*

She, who knows not the deep anguish of the sickness of my heart, despises my poor love, which her divine insight reads. O Káma! with thy five arrows, I thank thee, fare thou bravely, for thus raising in my soul this hope of her presence, which has withered ere it could bear its fruit!*

URVAŚÍ.

[*Looking at her companion.*

For shame! does the great King thus divine my thoughts? Again do I feel unable to stand before him, and reveal myself;—I will, therefore, write a line on this birch-leaf, which my power hath created for the occasion, and I will fling it in his way.

CHITRALEKHÁ.

I cordially approve your plan.

[URVAŚÍ *writes, and throws it on the ground.*

GRACIOSO.

Wonderful! oh, heavens! what can this be? Some snake's cast-off skin fallen on me to eat me up?

KING.

[*Looking.*

No snake's cast-off skin is this,—these are letters that are written on the birch-leaf.

* I have followed Lenz in interpreting this as ironical, but I have been obliged rather to expand it, to express the meaning.

GRACIOSO.

Can the lady Urvas'í, unseen by us, have heard your Highness' complaints, and written these letters on the birch-leaf, and flung it there, to testify her great love?

KING.

Nothing is impossible to the heavenly powers. *(He joyfully seizes and reads it.)* Oh, my friend! thy conjecture has come true!

GRACIOSO.

I long to hear what is written there!

URVAŚÍ.

[*Aside.*

Bravo! my worthy friend,—I admire your shrewdness.

KING.

Hear then.

[*He reads.*

"O my lord! as thou didst think of me, that I was ignorant of thy sorrow, so did I think of thee, who didst love me; and to me there hath been ever since no joy, as I rested on my couch of the sweet flowers of the coral-tree; and the very winds, as they blow through the groves of Nandana, to my fevered frame seem like fire."

URVAŚÍ.

[*To* CHITRALEKHÁ.

What does he say now?

CHITRALEKHÁ.

What, indeed, should he say, with his limbs thus faded, like the stalk of a lotus?

GRACIOSO.

Joy! your Highness' solace is like the initiatory rite at a sacrifice to me, when I am hungry.

KING.

Oh! why dost thou call it but a solace? Only look,—this leaf-borne declaration of my adored one, this messenger of her responding love, and pledge of the most desired possession, is as though my face, with open eyelids, were close to her's, with those eyes bright like wine!

URVAS'Í.

[*Aside.*

Here, indeed, our souls agree!

KING.

Ah, my friend, these letters are fading from the moisture of my hand,—take and hold my loved one's pledge in *thine.*

GRACIOSO.

What matters it? The lady Urvas'í has shown thee the blossom of thy desire, but she breaks her promise in the fruit.

URVAS'Í.

[*To* CHITRALEKHÁ.

Oh, dearest! while I collect myself from the agitation of standing so near him, do thou display thyself before him, and speak out what I approve.

CHITRALEKHÁ.

[*Advancing towards the* KING.

May the great King be ever victorious!

KING.

[*Starting at her sudden appearance, and in a courteous tone.*

Welcome to your highness! (*He looks at her side, as*

for another.) O happy one! thou dost not now so gladden my soul, thus coming without that friend of thine, like Yamuná, when parted from Gangá, if we had first seen it united.

CHITRALEKHÁ.

Do you not first have the line of clouds, and *then* the lightning?

GRACIOSO.

[*Aside.*

What is here? This new comer is not Urvas'í herself, but she must be her friend.

KING.

Take this seat, I pray.

CHITRALEKHÁ.

[*Seating herself.*

Urvas'í pays her obeisance to the King, and sends him this message........

KING.

What are her commands?

CHITRALEKHÁ.

"In that outrage offered by the Asura, the great King was my refuge, and now again when I am afflicted so sorely by the love that the sight of thee hath raised, the mighty monarch may well pity me again."

KING.

Ah, my friend! thou tellest that that lovely maiden sorrows, and seest thou not that Pururavas is feeling the same pang for her? Alike is our mutual passion,—oh! labour thou for us both; the heated iron must be welded to the heated iron.

CHITRALEKHÁ.

[*Returning to* URVAŚÍ.

O dearest! come hither; I have found your much dreaded Káma affable enough; and I am become the messenger from your beloved.

URVAŚÍ.

[*Trembling with sorrow and fear.*

Alas! perfidious! how lightly hast thou deserted me!

CHITRALEKHÁ.

[*Smiling.*

In this very next moment we shall know which of us will desert the other,—only keep up your spirits* meanwhile.

URVAŚÍ.

[*Coming forward with mingled fear and shame.*

May the great King be ever victorious!

KING.

[*Joyfully.*

Fairest lady! victory is already mine, when thy lips address me with that victorious title, thus transferred from the thousand-eyed Indra to a mortal!

[*He seizes her hand, and leads her to a seat.*

GRACIOSO.

What are your Highness' manners like? Is the King's friend, and he, too, a Bráhman, left unsaluted?

[URVAŚÍ *smiles and bows to him.*

* Such is Bopp's translation of the passage, in his *Glossarium Sanscritum*, p. 27: "*animus æquus, bene compositus.*"

GRACIOSO.

Health to your Highness!

(A Messenger of the Gods behind the scenes:)

Oh Chitralekhá! hasten Urvas'í away, for the Lord of the Winds, with the Guardians of the earth, is desirous, to-day, of beholding those dramatic love-scenes, which the sage Bharata made you skilled to perform,—those resting-places for the eight feelings of the soul.

[*They all listen,*—URVASÍ *shows distress.*

CHITRALEKHÁ.

Thou hast heard the words of the messenger; therefore take thy leave of the great King.

URVASÍ

[*Sighing.*

I have no power of utterance.

CHITRALEKHÁ.

O mighty monarch! Urvas'í addresses thee: "We are subjects," she says, "to the will of others; and I must bid thee farewell, to avoid offending the Monarch of the Devas."

KING.

[*With difficulty uttering his words.*

I would—not—interrupt your Lord's commands, but ye will not forget him whom ye leave behind!

URVASÍ *turns her face, full of sorrow at parting, towards the* KING, *and* exit *with her friend.*

KING.

[*With a sigh.*

Alas! now all the use of my eyes is gone!

GRACIOSO.

[*Wishing to show the leaf.*

But the birch-leaf——(*he stops in the middle of the sentence, and adds, confusedly, to himself:*) Hem! what's this? While I was gazing in my wonder at the sight of Urvas'í, that birch-leaf has unawares dropped from my hand!

KING.

What were you wishing to say, my friend?

GRACIOSO.

This, my lord, was the intended purport of my speech: let not your Highness be disheartened. Urvas'í's whole existence is now fast bound up in your own; though she has departed from hence, yet she cannot loosen the chain.

KING.

This very thing dwells in my mind, too; for methought, as she withdrew, though she be not under her own control, yet her free heart, manifest by the heaving of her bosom, seemed as though lodged within me by her sighs.

GRACIOSO.

Aside.

My heart trembles at the thought, how short the interval may be ere he drops some mention of the birch leaf!

KING.

My friend! with what diversion shall I solace my love-lorn mind? (*Recollecting suddenly.*) O! bring me the birch-leaf!

GRACIOSO.

[*Looking round with a woful countenance.*

Ha! how comes it to be out of sight? Surely it was a heavenly birch-leaf, and it must be gone after Urvas'í in her journey.

KING.

[*Reproachfully.*

Thou art always a thoughtless idiot!

GRACIOSO.

Let us look for it. (*Rising.*) Surely it must be here, or at any rate there! (*He dances about hither and thither.*)

Enter the QUEEN AÚŚÍNARÍ, *with her* SERVANT *and royal retinue.*

QUEEN.

Tell me, Nipuniká! did you really see the King going into the creeper-bower, accompanied by Mánavaka?

NIPUNIKÁ.

Have I ever given your Highness false information before?

QUEEN.

[*Walking round, and looking before her.*

O Nipuniká! what is this leaf, like a strip of fresh bark, which the south wind has blown hither?

NIPUNIKÁ.

[*Observing it.*

Oh, my lady! it has letters on it, though I cannot

distinguish them, from its turning round and round; but see! it is caught in your anklet; shall I read its contents?

[*Seizing it.*

QUEEN.

Look into it first; I will listen if it contain nothing unseemly.

NIPUNIKÁ.

[*Having done so.*

Oh, my lady! here is that rumour all open now. I suspect that these are some love-lines from Urvas'í to the King; it has, doubtless, fallen into our hands through Mánavaka's carelessness.

QUEEN.

Well, seize their meaning.

[NIPUNIKÁ *reads it.*

QUEEN.

Come! let us go and see our nymph-lover, and take this with us as our present.

NIPUNIKÁ.

As your Highness commands.

KING.

O thou divine breeze of Malaya! friend of the Spring! bear thou away, for thy perfume, the collected odorous dust of the flowers of thc creepers; but what hast thou to do with this stolen letter, which my loved one's affection hath written? Thou knowest that those who are pained with love are sustained by a hundred such pleasures as these, when their hearts have no hope to rest upon, that they shall soon attain their desires.

NIPUNIKÁ.

Oh, my mistress! look—look! there is a search going on for this very birch-leaf of ours.

QUEEN.

Let us, then, meanwhile, watch him — stand thou by in silence.

GRACIOSO.

[*To the* KING.

See! what is this? Ah! I have been deceived by the tail of a peacock, which shone like a blue lotus in full blossom.

KING.

Luckless wretch that I am;—I am on all sides undone!

QUEEN.

[*Suddenly advancing.*

My lord! you have troubled yourself enough—here is the birch-leaf!

KING.

[*In great confusion, and to himself.*

What! the Queen! *(Abashed.)* Welcome to your Highness!

QUEEN.

It has been "*ill-come*," to me, at the present moment.

KING.

[*Aside to the* GRACIOSO.

Oh, my friend! what is to be done?

GRACIOSO.

Little, indeed, has the thief to say, when the stolen goods are the evidence that detects him.

KING.

It was not this leaf which I sought; it was the leaf of a Mantra* for which this search was commenced.

QUEEN.

It is well to conceal one's good fortune.

GRACIOSO.

Let be—hasten a banquet for him; he will be well when his bile is abated.

QUEEN.

See, Nipuniká! how well the Bráhman counsels his friend! what else, indeed, could a sick heart wish for?

GRACIOSO.

But only consider, how naturally all men are soothed by a banquet!

KING.

You fool! you perforce add to my distress, when I have already offended too much.

QUEEN.

No, indeed! it is not your Highness that has offended! I am the offending party, since I have intruded where my presence was unwelcome. Nipuniká, let us be gone!

[*She turns angrily away.*

KING.

Alas! I am the guilty; O fairest one! be appeased and relent from thy wrath; the mistress of the house is angry, and how can the servant seem faultless?

[*He falls at her feet.*

* A portion of the Vedas.

QUEEN.

O deceiver! my heart is not so credulous as to trust in the homage you offer. I fear you when you are so kind and penitent.

NIPUNIKÁ.

Will your Highness walk this way?

[*The* QUEEN *leaves the* KING *and exit with her retinue.*

GRACIOSO.

The Queen has departed, troubled, like a rain-swollen torrent! Rise, therefore, rise!

KING.

Oh, my friend! it has failed—only see; a lover's salutation, with words of affection, but without affection itself, enters not the skilled woman's heart, like the gem that has only factitious colours.

GRACIOSO.

Your Highness' words are kind; but the opthalmic patient cannot endure the light of the lamp immediately in front of him.

KING.

Oh, speak not thus;—though my heart be with Urvas'í, yet I still feel a deep respect for the Queen; but since she has rejected my salutation, I will arm myself with firmness against her.

GRACIOSO.

Well! let the conversation about her stand still awhile; I am dying with hunger, and it is for your Highness to keep me alive. Lo! it is time to bathe and to dine!

KING.

[*Looking upward.*

What! is the half of the day already gone? It is for this, then, that the peacock, oppressed with the heat, now sits in the cool basin at the foot of the tree; the bees have penetrated the blossoms of the Karnikára, and are slumbering there; leaving the heated water, the waterfowl repairs to the lotus-bed by the shore; and the wearied parrot begs for water in that house of his sports—his cage!*

[*Exeunt.*

* This line seems literally, "The cage-parrot, inhabiting his house of sports."

END OF THE SECOND ACT.

ACT III.

Enter TWO DISCIPLES OF BHARATA.

FIRST DISCIPLE.

Oh, my friend Pailava, when our preceptor went from the cell of the holy fire to great Indra's palace, he bade you take a seat with him in his chariot, while I was left behind to guard the cell; I would, therefore, now ask you—was the heavenly audience pleased or not with our Guru's dramatic performance?

SECOND DISCIPLE.

How much it was pleased, I know not; but most assuredly during the performance of the play, "*The Choice of Lakshmí*," which Saraswatí herself had composed, Urvas'í wholly lost herself in some of the impassioned parts!

FIRST DISCIPLE.

There was a fault manifest—this is what you were going to say.

SECOND DISCIPLE.

Yes, indeed! she actually broke down in her part.

FIRST DISCIPLE.

How so?

SECOND DISCIPLE.

Urvas'í sustained the part of Lakshmí, and on her being addressed by Menaká, who played in the character of

Varuní:—"The guardian spirits of the three worlds, with Kes'ava, are assembled together,—on whom is thy heart fixed?"——

FIRST DISCIPLE.

And what then?

SECOND DISCIPLE.

She ought to have answered, "*On Purushottama*" but, "*On Pururavas*" escaped from her lips, instead.

FIRST DISCIPLE.

Ah! our organs of intellect are obedient to destiny! But was not the sage angry with her?

SECOND DISCIPLE.

Our preceptor cursed her, but Indra showed favour to her.

FIRST DISCIPLE.

How so?

SECOND DISCIPLE.

"Forasmuch as thou hast gone counter to my instructions, therefore shall thy heavenly knowledge utterly fail." Such was the preceptor's ban. However, when Indra saw poor Urvasí standing with her face bent down in utter shame, he thus spoke to her,—"To him, the holy King, in whom thy being is bound up, I owe gratitude as having been my ally in battle; therefore dwell thou with Pururavas, as thou desirest, until that he has offspring from thee."

FIRST DISCIPLE.

The speech was worthy of great Indra, who knows the heart's inmost thoughts.

SECOND DISCIPLE.

[*Looking at the sun.*

In our eager discourse we have transgressed the hour of ablution; let us, therefore, hasten to our preceptor's side.

[*Exeunt.*

END OF THE VISHKAMBHAKA.

Enter the CHAMBERLAIN.

CHAMBERLAIN.

Every father of a family strives in the proper time of life to attain wealth, but afterwards his sons relieve him of his burden, and he betakes himself to rest; but ours has been a growing old which day by day impairs our standing in life, until our very voice be changed from the sorrow of the servitude! 'Tis a tiresome business—this charge over women! I have received the following commission from her Highness, the daughter of the King of Kás'í, who has undertaken a vow:—"Go," she says, "and carry my former message again to the King, in which I dismissed my pride, and begged him, by the mouth of Nipuniká, to come to the completion of my vow." I will see the King when he has completed the evening ceremonies. *(He walks round and looks.)* Sweet are the tidings of the close of day to the palace! The peacocks sit strewn on their poles lazy with sleep; the doves, as they fly to their turret tops, can scarce be distinguished from the fumes of incense which escape from the windows; and the old men of the seraglio, engaged in their duties, are distributing the lighted lamps for the evening rites on the spots decked with offerings of flowers. (*Looking.*) Ah! here comes his Majesty! Lo! yonder he shines, surrounded by the torches in the hands of the maidens who attend him,—like a moving mountain, whose wings have not been cut off,* with a garland of the Karnikára in full bloom, hung along its sides! I will watch and keep him in view.

Enter the KING, *as described, with his retinue and the* GRACIOSO.

KING.

[*To himself.*

My sorrows have been lost in occupation, and I have thus managed without extreme difficulty to wile away the day; but how shall I ever pass the night with no diversion to break the long monotony of its watches?

CHAMBERLAIN.

[*Advancing.*

May the King be ever victorious! The Queen sends this message to your Majesty:—"The moon is beautiful behind the Palace of the Gem; there let your Highness stay awhile, and watch until the moon enters its asterism Rohiní."

* Such is the explanation of *apakshasádát*, given by the Scholiast, as quoted in Lenz' Appendix, p. 18. The wings of the mountains are the clouds; they are said to have been cut off by Indra. See *Meghadúta* (Wilson), p. 7.

KING.

Tell the Queen that it shall be as she desires.

[*Exit* CHAMBERLAIN, *promising compliance.*

KING.

[*To the* GRACIOSO.

Oh, my friend! is this undertaking of the Queen's really on account of a vow?

GRACIOSO.

I conjecture that her Highness feels some compunction, and now desires, under the pretext of this vow, to efface her scornful rejection of your salutation.

KING.

You speak plausibly. Wise women, when they have rejected kind greetings, on second thoughts feel remorse, and they distress themselves with various expedients to to pacify their beloved. Come, show the way behind the Palace of the Gem.

GRACIOSO.

This way, this way; let your Highness ascend by this staircase of crystal, cold with Gangá's spray; the Palace of the Gem is lovely at every season.

[*The* KING *and all ascend.*

GRACIOSO.

[*Looking.*

The moon must be close at hand, for the eastern quarter is escaping from darkness, and assuming a reddening hue.

KING.

You think rightly. The darkness is scattered further and further by the rays of the moon, though still hidden below the horizon; and Indra's* quarter gladdens my eyes as though it were a human countenance parting the locks from its forehead.

GRACIOSO.

O see! O see! The lord of the Oshadí plants† is now risen—bright, like granulated sugar!

KING.

[*Smiling.*

The objects of the glutton are always something eatable! *(Folding his hands and bowing.)* O divine Monarch of the stars! thou that bringest light to the rites of the good, and gladdenest the manes and the Suras with ambrosia, and dispellest the shadows that gather in the night,—O thou that art set on Śiva's crest,—Hail to thee! all Hail!

GRACIOSO.

By a sign declared to a Bráhman like me, I know that your grandfather‡ has favourably dismissed you; be seated, I pray; I shall then sit happily too.

* Indra's quarter is the East. Wilson only gives Garuda as the meaning of *harivâhana*. Bopp, in his Glossary, translates it Indra, *i.e.*, *flavos equos habens*, and so, too, the Scholiast. The word rendered *horizon*, in the previous sentence, properly means the eastern mountain behind which the sun and moon are supposed to rise.

† "*Littéralement*, 'Le maître des herbes, le roi de la végetation.'" —Chézy. Compare Deuteronomy xxxiii., 14, "The precious things put forth by the moon."

‡ Pururavas was of the Lunar race. The moon, in Sanscrit, is masculine.

KING.

[*Accepting his invitation and looking round on his attendants.*

Our lamps are superfluous and lost in the moonlight; ye can retire to rest.

ATTENDANTS.

As the King commands. [*Exeunt.*

KING.

[*To the* GRACIOSO, *and looking at the Moon.*

Yet a moment, my friend, and her Highness will be here; while we are still alone, I will tell thee my present state.

GRACIOSO.

Ah! no Urvas'í is visible here; but since we have witnessed her reciprocal affection, you may well support yourself by hope.

KING.

It is so; great, indeed is the anguish of my soul; but —like a river's current, whose dashing stream is hemmed in by rugged rocks, so — though the joy of union be obstructed,—my love still bounds onwards, following its native impulse.

GRACIOSO.

Inasmuch as you are still so handsome, for all that your limbs are so wasted,—I foresee therefrom a speedy meeting with the nymphs.

KING.

[*As though hailing an omen.*

My right arm comforts me, in my heavy sorrow, with its throbbings, just as you have done with your hope-inspiring words.

GRACIOSO.

A Bráhman's words are never other than true.

[*The* KING *sits, with a hopeful look, and then enters in the air* URVAŚÍ, *in a gala dress,* attended by* CHITRALEKHÁ.

URVAŚÍ.

[*Looking at herself.*

Dear friend! this dress of mine, decorated with pearl ornaments, and trimmed with sapphires, pleases my heart.

CHITRALEKHÁ.

Words cannot praise it enough; I can only think, "Would that I were Pururavas!"

URVAŚÍ.

Alas! I have no power in myself; do you, with all speed, bring him here, or take me to his dwelling.

CHITRALEKHÁ.

We are come to the glorious palace of your beloved, like the peak of Kailása reflected in the dark Yamuná's waters.†

URVAŚÍ.

Put forth your heavenly power and learn where is the King who hath stolen my heart away, and on what he is engaged?

* *Literally.* 'Dressed as a woman who goes to meet her lover.'

† Compare *Meghadúta*, Sloke 53.

CHITRALEKHÁ.

[*To herself.*

Well stay—I will jest with her awhile. *(Aloud).* I see him, dearest; he is standing yonder at a time fit for enjoyment, enjoying the pleasure of the desired society of a friend.

URVAŚÍ.

Away! my heart will not believe it. O dear Chitralekhá! you have got something in your head when you speak thus. Surely it is only the society of that friend who was with him before,* when he carried off my heart as I left.

CHITRALEKHÁ.

[*Looking.*

Behold the holy monarch himself, alone with his friend in the Palace of the Gem. Let us approach him.

[*They descend.*

KING.

[*To the* GRACIOSO.

Oh, my friend! the pain of love increases with the night.

URVAŚÍ.

[*To* CHITRALEKHÁ.

My heart trembles at these ambiguous words. Let us remain unseen, and listen to his conversation, until our uncertainties are dispelled.

CHITRALEKHÁ.

As you please.

GRACIOSO.

You should enjoy the ambrosia-laden moonbeams.

* *"Coram hoc ipso amicali, quem dicis, conventu scilicet cor mihi ab illo rapiebatur."*—LENZ.

KING.

Oh, my friend! this sickness is not to be cured with such means as these; 'tis not the fresh couch of flowers, nor the moonbeams, nor the unguent of sandal poured over all the body, nor strings of pearls;—she, the heavenly maiden, alone can drive my love-melancholy away, or only secret converse, flying to her as its subject, can lighten my heart.

URVAŚÍ.

Oh, my heart! this is the fruit thou hast gained for having left me and flown hither!

GRACIOSO.

Ah! I also, when I cannot obtain curds and sugar or sugar-cane, make myself happy with thinking about it.

KING.

You, however, soon find *your* desires!

GRACIOSO.

And you, too, ere long shall obtain *her!*

KING.

My friend, this is what I think——

CHITRALEKHÁ.

[*To* URVAŚÍ.

Listen! O discontented one!

GRACIOSO.

What is it?

KING.

This limb, which was pressed by hers, in the shaking of the chariot, alone of all my limbs retains its power to act; the rest of my body is but a dead weight on the earth.

URVAŚÍ.

Why should I longer delay? (*Approaching hurriedly.*) O dear Chitralekhá! alas! the King regards me not, even though I stand in his presence.

CHITRALEKHÁ.

[*Smiling.*

Oh, impatient one! thou hast not thrown off thy veil.

A VOICE BEHIND THE SCENES.

"This way, O Queen!"

[*All listen.* URVAŚÍ *and her friend look dismayed.*

GRACIOSO.

[*Surprised.*

Good heavens! the Queen approaches; put a seal on thy lips.

KING.

Do you, too, sit with your face's expression veiled.

URVAŚÍ.

Oh, my friend! what is to be done?

CHITRALEKHÁ.

Cease this alarm, thou art still invisible; the Queen is seen here in fulfilment of a vow; she will not stay long.

Enter the QUEEN, *with her* ATTENDANTS, *bearing gifts.*

QUEEN.

[*Looking at the moon.*

Still fairer seems the moon from its meeting with its asterism Rohiní.

FEMALE SERVANT.

Thus, too, will there be increased splendour to the King when your Highness has joined him.

[*They walk round.*

GRACIOSO.

[*To the* KING.

Ah! now I understand it all; she comes to offer the *swastiváchana*, or else she has dismissed her wrath against you,* under the pretext of a vow to the moon; to my eyes, her Highness looks very beautiful to-day.

KING.

[*Smiling.*

In either case your last remark appears to me true, for her Highness with her white garments, and adorned only with white mangala† flowers, and her forehead decked with the stalks of the striped *durbá* grass, seems, indeed, now fully appeased, and her form has dismissed all its haughtiness under the pretext of her vow.

QUEEN.

[*Advancing.*

May the son of a noble father‡ be ever victorious!

ATTENDANTS.

May our Lord be victorious!

GRACIOSO.

Health to your Highness!

KING.

Welcome, O goddess!

[*He seizes her hand and leads her to a seat.*

* The Scholiast explains *bhavantam antarena*, by *bhavantam uddis'ya.*

† *Panicum dactylon.*

‡ *i.e.*, in theatrical language, a husband.

URVAŚÍ.

Well may she be addressed with the title of goddess; she yields not even to Sachí in beauty.

CHITRALEKHÁ.

What! can you talk of a rival's face?

QUEEN.

I have to accomplish a certain vow under your Highness' auspices; I pray you bear with the inconvenience a moment.

KING.

O Mánavaka! the inconvenience is a favour.

GRACIOSO.

Would that I might often have such inconvenience as this, while performing the rites of the *swastiváchana*.

KING.

Under what name is your Highness' vow?

[*The* QUEEN *looks at* NIPUNIKÁ.

NIPUNIKÁ.

It is called "The Conciliation of a Husband's regard."

KING.

[*Looking at the* QUEEN.

O virtuous one! with this vow night and day you weary your body, tender as a lotus-stalk; why is your slave to be thus conciliated, who himself is pining with desire for your favour?

URVAŚÍ.

[*With a forced smile.*

What a great respect he has for her!

CHITRALEKHÁ.

Hush, O foolish one! courtiers flatter most when their hearts are elsewhere.

QUEEN.

It is all through the efficacy of this vow that my husband is so touched.

GRACIOSO.

[*To the* KING.

Be still, my Lord! it is not seemly to contradict the words of our friends.

QUEEN.

Maidens! bring hither the gifts, that I may pay my homage to the moonbeams, as they fall on the palace.

ATTENDANTS.

As the Queen commands. Here are the gifts!

QUEEN.

Present them. (*She worships the moonbeams, with offerings of flowers, etc.*) Honour also with these sweetmeats the venerable Mánavaka and the Chamberlain.

ATTENDANTS.

As the Queen commands. O venerable Mánavaka! these propitiatory gifts are for *thee.*

GRACIOSO.

[*Taking the dish.*

Prosperity to your Highness! may your vow be very successful.

NIPUNIKÁ.

And these are for thee, O venerable Chamberlain!

CHAMBERLAIN.

[*Taking them.*

Prosperity to your Highness!

QUEEN.

Come hither, my Lord, for a moment.

KING.

Here I am.

QUEEN.

[*Folding her hands, in token of homage to the* KING, *and bowing.*

Having called to witness yonder twins of heaven, the Moon and Rohiní, I thus conciliate my husband,—Whosoever she be, whom my lord loves, and who herself desires my lord's society, with her henceforth shall he dwell without let or hindrance from me!

URVAŚÍ.

Wonderful, indeed! I know not what more she will say; but my heart is now brightened with confidence.

CHITRALEKHÁ.

O dearest! thy union with thy beloved has been consented to by the noble Queen, faithful to her husband, and it will now meet with no obstacle.

GRACIOSO.

[*Aside.*

When a man has his hands cut off, and the culprit flies before him, no wonder if he says, "Go! go! you shall this time have impunity!"* *(Aloud.)* Has the King, then, neglected your Highness lately?

QUEEN.

Fool! I desire my Lord's happiness, even though it be by the end of my own. Judge hence, then, if he be dear to me or not.

KING.

O jealous one! thou hast all power over me to give me to another, or keep me as thy slave; but, indeed, timid one, my love towards thee is not as thou suspectest.

QUEEN.

Well, let it be! The vow of conciliation has been fulfilled, as prescribed. Come, my attendants, let us depart.

KING.

You will not leave me reconciled, if you depart so soon.

QUEEN.

My lord! the sanctity of the vow is now inviolate.

[*Exit with her train.*

URVAŚÍ.

The King seems to love her, yet I cannot call back my heart.

CHITRALEKHÁ.

How, indeed, can hope so firm as your's be called back?

* This is Lenz's translation. Professor Wilson gives it very differently, "The culprit that escapes before his hand is cut off, determines never to run such a risk again."

KING.

[*Returning to his seat.*

My friend! is her Highness far away?

GRACIOSO.

Say freely what you wish. She has soon left you as a doctor leaves his sick patient, having decided that he is incurable.

KING.

Oh! would that Urvas'í....

URVASÍ.

[*To herself.*

To-day he will attain his desire.

KING.

....Might but secretly let fall in my ear the sweet sound of her anklets, or, softly stealing behind me, might cover my eyes with her lotus hand! Oh! would that she might descend in this palace, and while lingering, delayed through fear, be perforce led towards me, step by step, by her dexterous friend!

CHITRALEKHÁ.

O dear Urvas'í! pray now fulfil this desire of his.

URVASÍ.

[*Timidly.*

I will sport with him a moment.

[*She steps behind him and covers his eyes, while* CHITRALEKHÁ *makes the* GRACIOSO *conscious of it.*

KING.

[*Starting at the touch.*

My friend! is not the fair thigh-born daughter of Nárâyana here?

GRACIOSO.

How does your Highness know it?

KING.

What else can it be? How otherwise, from this touch, should I feel a thrill through each hair of my body? The lotus opens not at the sun's beams, as at the moon's.

URVAŚÍ.

Strange to say! both my hands are fixed as with adamantine glue. I cannot draw them away! *(She half-closes her eyes, and having taken her hands away, stands frightened. She slowly advances.)* May the King be victorious!

CHITRALEKHÁ.

All joy to thee, my brother!*

KING.

It has already come.

URVAŚÍ.

O Chitralekhá! the Queen has given him to me; therefore, as loving him, I approach his person. Oh! I beseech you, think not that I claimed him before my right.

GRACIOSO.

What! were you here when the sun set?†

* Such seems the force of *vayasya* here. See Lenz, note 77.

† *i.e.*, and heard the Queen's words.

KING.

[*Looking on* URVAŚÍ.

If the gift of the Queen is the claim you put in for my person, by whose consent, then, did you steal away my heart before?

CHITRALEKHÁ.

O King! she hath nothing to reply. Let my words now, I pray you, be heard.

KING.

I am attentive.

CHITRALEKHÁ.

Immediately after the Spring, through the hot season, I am required in attendance on the Sun; I beseech my brother, therefore, to take all care that my loved companion may never the while regret the Swarga she hath left.

GRACIOSO.

What, in sooth, is there in Swarga, to be remembered? There it is neither eaten nor drunken, but they are only intent upon being like fishes—with unwinking eyes!

KING.

Oh, my friend! how shall she be ever made to forget Swarga, with its indescribable joys? But be assured that Pururavas will be her slave, and no other woman shall share him.

CHITRALEKHÁ.

I am, indeed, favoured. Dear Urvaśí! be of good cheer, and bid me farewell.

URVAŚÍ.

[*In a sad voice embracing her.*

Dearest! thou wilt not forget me?

CHITRALEKHÁ.

[*Smiling.*

It is you that ought to be asked that question by me, now that you are united to your beloved.

[*She bows to the* KING, *and exit.*

GRACIOSO.

Joy! joy! may your Highness be blessed with the fulfilment of his desires!

KING.

Behold, this is the fulfilment! When I attained the empire of the world, with its one canopy,* and its footstool gorgeous with the gems of the diadems of neighbouring kings, yet was I not so blessed as I am this day, when the dear right is mine of doing her commands as a slave at her feet!

URVAŚÍ.

I have no power of speech to say more.

KING.

[*Having taken hold of her.*

Oh, how void of all obstacle is this present fulness of possession of my desires! These moonbeams verily gladden

* *Literally.* 'With one umbrella.'

my body; love's arrows themselves are propitious to my heart, and all that erst seemed stern with wrath, oh, loveliest lady! is reconciled to me through my union with thee.

URVAŚÍ.

I have erred against my King in tarrying so long.

KING.

Oh, lovely one! say not so. That which seemed sorrow while it was near, after the interval of a year is joy; the shadow of the tree is most a rest to him who hath been scorched by the noon.

GRACIOSO.

Noble lady! we have enjoyed the moonbeams, so delicious at evening. It is time for thee to enter thy home.

KING.

Do thou, therefore, shew the way to thy new friend.

GRACIOSO.

This way, your Highness.

[*He walks round.*

KING.

Oh, lovely one! this is now my desire . . . .

URVAŚÍ.

What is it?

KING.

Before, when the object of my love was unattained, the night passed as if lengthened an hundred-fold. Oh, happy indeed shall I be, maiden with the fair brow, if it passes at the same rate *now* thou art here!

[*Exeunt.*

END OF THE THIRD ACT.

ACT IV.

Introductory song (Akshiptiká) of SAHAJANYÁ *and* CHITRALEKHÁ, *behind the scenes.*

Forlorn, in separation from her best beloved, she flutters, bewildered, with one of her companions, on the bosom of the lake, with its sun-lotus-blossoms, opened at the touch of the sunbeams.

Enter SAHAJANYÁ *and* CHITRALEKHÁ.

CHITRALEKHÁ.

[*As she enters and looks round, in the Dwipadiká measure.*

Consumed with sorrow for their friend, the loving pair of swans mourn in the lake, with their eyes flowing with tears.

SAHAJANYÁ.

[*Mournfully.*

Dear Chitralekhá! the shade on thy face, dark like the fading lotus, betrays the sickness of thy heart; oh, tell me the cause of thy sadness, that I, too, may be a like sorrower with thee.

CHITRALEKHÁ.

[*In a sorrowful voice.*

Oh, my friend! I have been full of longing regrets, since I saw the spring-season arrive without her my loved friend, who had been appointed for attendance on the sun, in the order of the service of the nymphs.

SAHAJANYÁ.

I know well your mutual fondness, but what further?

CHITRALEKHÁ.

And at this very time, while I fixed my thoughts in divine meditation to see what tidings there might be, a terrible misfortune indeed have I found!

SAHAJANYÁ.

What can it be?

CHITRALEKHÁ.

[*Mournfully.*

Urvas'í, then, had taken the fortunate king (who had entrusted the burden of his kingdom to his counsellors), and was gone to roam with him in the Gandha-mâdana forests, in the region of the heights of Kailása.

SAHAJANYÁ.

[*Applauding.*

It was a pleasure which right well suited such spots! but what more?

CHITRALEKHÁ.

There, on the banks of the Mandákiní, my loved Urvas'í was deeply incensed, because the king for a moment directed his thoughts to the daughter of a Vidyádhara, named Udakavatí, who was sporting on the hills of sand.

SAHAJANYÁ.

She was jealous, and her love went too far. Well, destiny was strong even there; what followed?

CHITRALEKHÁ.

She rejected all her husband's conciliations, and her heart being blinded by the Sage's curse, she forgot the divine decree and hurried into the grove of Kartikeya, to be for ever shunned by all damsels; and immediately on her entrance, her form was changed into that of a creeper growing by the edge of the wood.

SAHAJANYÁ.

[*In great distress.*

Surely there is nothing which is inviolable to destiny, by which even the change of such a form can be wrought. But what more?

CHITRALEKHÁ.

The King, utterly reft of his senses, wanders through the forest, ever seeking his beloved, and spends days and nights in continual exclamations, "Urvas'í is here!—Urvas'í is there!" *(Looking at the sky.)* And little cure, I conjecture, will he find from yonder rising of clouds, which wakes a longing even in the blest.*

* The "Rainy Season" of the Hindú poet answers to our Spring, being as full of tender associations.

[JAMBHALIKÁ SONG]

Consumed with sorrow for their friend, the loving pair of swans mourn in the lake, their hot tears ceaselessly welling.

SAHAJANYÁ.

O dearest! is there any means of re-union?

CHITRALEKHÁ.

Alas! whence, indeed, is there any means, except from the jewel of union which sprang from the glow of Durga's feet?

SAHAJANYÁ.

Oh! surely such noble forms do not long have sorrow as their portion; some means of re-union, I foretell, will be assuredly discovered, which shall conciliate her favour again. *(Looking at the eastern quarter.)* But come, let us haste to our attendance on the sun, yon glorious monarch of the east.

[KHANDADHÁRA SONG]

Agitated with anguish of heart, longing for the sight of her companion—amidst the soul-ravishing splendours of the full-blown lotuses, wanders along the lake the lonely swan.

[*Exeunt.*

END OF THE PRAVEŚAKA.

Behind the Scenes, an Introductory Song of PURURAVAS.

The lord of elephants enters the forest—how visibly changed, with the madness of separation from his love, while his mountain-form is adorned with flowers and sprays, the spoils of the trees which he passes.

Enter the KING, *mad, with his gaze fixed on the sky.*

KING.

[*Angrily.*

Ah, villain, demon! stay! stay! whither fliest thou with my darling? (*Looking.*) What! he hath flown from the summit of the mountain to the sky, and now pelts me with arrows. (*Seizing a clod of earth in his hand, and running as if to strike, he breaks out immediately in the Dwipadiká* measure, looking on all sides.*)

[SONG]

With a pang fixed in his heart for the loss of his love, and flapping his wings, in the lake mourns the young swan, with tear-streams gushing from his eyes.

(*Suddenly recognising the object, in a wailing voice*). Ah no! it is yon shower-armed cloud, and no haughty demon of the night; it is yonder bow of heaven drawn to its full, and no bow for earthly arrows; it is yon keen-shafted shower, and not a succession of arrows; it is the lightning glistening like a streak of gold on the touch-stone,† and not

* This and other similar terms used throughout this Act refer to musical measures; but their precise import is doubtful.

† Kálidása repeats this simile in the *Meghadúta*, sloke 39.

my own loved Urvas'i! (*He falls fainting—again he rises with a sigh—in Dwipadiká.*) Now I know too well some demon of darkness steals away her of the fawn-like eye, when yonder dark cloud carries off the young lightning! (*Having thought a moment—in a mournful voice.*) Where—where then can she be gone? Perhaps she has hidden herself somewhere in her displeasure, by an effort of her heavenly power; yet she will not be angry long; perhaps she may have flown up to Swarga; yet still her soul is full of tenderness towards me! (*Angrily.*) If she were now before me, not all the enemies of the gods could carry her away. What means it, then, that she is now gone so far out of my sight? (*Looking round, sighing and weeping—in Dwipadiká.*) Ah! to those who have adverse fortune, sorrow comes fast bound to sorrow; do you ask me, how so? See—this blow of separation from my beloved so hard to be endured and fallen so suddenly upon me; and that, too, when the days are so delightful, that we need no umbrella to shade us from the heat through the rising of the new water-laden clouds. (*Charcharí air.*) Restrain thy anger at my command, O cloud, that overspreadest the sky with thy continuous showers; if ever in my wanderings o'er the earth I behold my beloved, then, oh then, whatsoever thou shalt do I will bear it. (*After musing—in Charchariká*). Alas! the redoubled sorrow of my mind is all beheld in vain. But since the holy sages say, that the king is the source of seasons, shall I put back the season of the rainy clouds?

[CHARCHARÍ SONG]

Resonant with the songs of the perfume-maddened bees, and the loudly-blown pipes of the Kokilas, with its multitude of young branches shaken by the wind which sweeps through them,—with various gestures of joy, dances the heavenly tree.*

(*He dances to the song.*) But I will not put the season back, after all! since it now pays me homage as its liege, with all the signs of the Rainy Season. (*Smiling.*) Yes—yonder cloud is my canopy of state, bright with streaks of lightning for gold, and the Nichula trees wave over me their sprays for chowries; my heralds are yonder peacocks, as they raise their shriller voices at the cessation of the heat; and the mountains are my merchants, busied in bringing me their showers. (*Again, Charcharí.*) Well, but what have I to do with the homage of a court-train? I will wander away through the wood and seek for the darling I have lost.

[BHINNAKA SONG]

[*In the interval of recitation.*†

Bereft of his love, and intensely distressed, behold! with worn feet, the lord of the elephant-herd slowly roams, followed by the pangs of absence, in the forests of the hills, blazing with blossom!

* The *Kalpa* in Indra's heaven.

† The Scholiast explains *páthá* as "instrumental symphony," and reads *páthasyánte*. But why may we not take it in its usual sense of "recitation," applying it to the King's monologue (to which the verb *patha* is applied, p. 45, l. 17; and p. 46, l. 18); and thus supposing that the songs were sung behind the scenes, in the intervals of silence?

(*Having walked round and looked, joyfully, in Dwipadiká measure*). Ah! ah! my resolve has prospered! This young Banana, and its flowers, with their red edges and their moist calyxes,* recals the memory of her eyes, when anger suffused them with tears. She is gone from hence, but how shall she be tracked? If she with the fair form had touched with her feet the cloud-watered soil of these woods, I should see the line of her lovely footsteps marked with lac, with the deeper impression of her heels behind. (*He walks round and looks—in Dwipadiká.*) Ah! ah! I have found a sign by which my angry love's way is joyfully tracked: without doubt, this is her scarf, dark blue like a parrot's breast, which she threw in anger away, when it impeded her path, and it yet bears the marks of her falling tear-drops, which have stolen the redness of her lips. Well! I will seize it. (*Walking round, and perceiving what it is, with tears*). What! it is but a grassy glade covered with Indragopas! whence, then, in this forest shall I find any tidings of my love! (*Looking.*) Perched on the rocky cliff of the mountain, with a shower hanging over it, yon peacock sits gazing at the clouds, with its tail shaken by the strong east wind, and its neck stretched out to its full, as swelling with its coming cry. Well, I will ask it.

[KHANDAKA SONG]

Full of sorrow, longing for the sight of his

* Or perhaps, "laden with moisture."

beloved, the noblest of elephants, the repeller of enemies, wanders hurriedly on, bewildered in his inmost mind.

(*Charcharí—in the interval of the Khandaka.*) I beseech thee, O lord of the Peacocks! tell me, if, as thou roamest through the woods, thou hast seen my own beautiful bride. O hear me! a face like the moon, and a Hansa's gait; thou wilt know the signs of her, for I have told them unto thee. (*He sits down with Charchariká music, and folds his hands.*) O bird of the white-angled eye, with the dark-blue throat! hast thou seen in this forest the desire of my heart, my loved wife, with the long eye,*—an object well worthy to be seen? (*He sits with Charchariká music, and looks.*) Ha! he gives me no answer, but begins to dance. (*Again Charchari.*) What can be the reason of his delight? Ha! I know it. Now that my loved one is lost, his tail beautiful like a cloud, outspread in the gentle breeze, is without a rival; for whom, indeed, would the peacock charm, if *she* were near, with the flower-encircled tresses of her, the lovely-haired, fallen all loose in the hour of joy? Well; I will ask no more of one who thus rejoices over other's ills. (*He looks round with a Dwipadiká air.*) Ah! yonder is a female Kokila sitting on the boughs of the rose-apple, her passion inflamed, now the sultry heat is past. These are the wisest of birds. I will ask it.

* *Literally.* "With the long corner of the eye."

[KHURAKA SONG.]

Dwelling in the grove of the Vidyádharas, with tears of sadness bursting from his eyes, and with all the joy of his heart driven far away, the King of Elephants wanders on and on, with the majesty of a cloud.*

(*After the Khuraka a Charcharí.*) Oh, alien-reared Kokila with the sweet song! tell me, O dweller in foreign nests! has my fair beloved been seen by thee, wandering at will through this Nandana grove? (*Having danced, he advances with Balantiká, and kneels.*) Thee lovers call the messenger of Love; thou art his unerring dart, skilled to humble pride,—oh! either bring her, my loved one, before me, or quickly lead me, Bird of the sweet note! wherever she may be. (*Having moved a little to the left.*†) What saidst thou? Didst thou ask why she has forsaken one so devoted as I? (*Looking forward.*) Oh, honoured bird! she was angry; but I cannot call to mind a single act of mine, that could cause her wrath; the tyranny of women over their lovers waits not for intentional offences.‡ (*He sits down in agitation, and then kneels, repeating, "she was angry" and looks.*) What! she interrupts my discourse, and only thinks of her own concerns; but well runs the proverb, "Men say that

* I follow Wilson and Lenz in translating *ambara* as "a cloud,"—it properly means "the sky."

† *A'kás'e* is simply a stage-direction, implying—said to a person out of sight. See Wilson's *Lexicon*.

‡ The Scholiast explains *bháva* by *abhipráya*.

the greatest ill of another's is utterly cold to themselves;" since yonder bird, unheeding my love, now I am fallen into adversity! is absorbed in sipping the royal rose-apple's newly-ripened fruit, as a woman blinded with the intoxication of love, her lover's lip. They are both gone—the fair songstress as well as my beloved; I will not be angry—may she dwell in joy. I will follow her. (*Having risen, he walks round, with Dwipadiká, and looks.*) Ah! yonder to the right, by the edge of the wood, I hear the sound of anklets, that tell of the motion of my beloved one's feet. I will follow it.

[SONG]

[*Six Upabhangas in the Kakubha mode.*

His face forlorn for the absence of his beloved; his eyes troubled with the incessant welling of tears; his feet tottering under his insupportable anguish; his whole body consumed by the mighty pain that pervades him, and his mind more and more racked with anguish, and greatly terrified,*—roams through the wood, the Elephant-King.

[*He looks all round—with Dwipadiká.*

[SONG]

Parted from his loved mate, consumed with the flame of intense sorrow, and his eyes blinded with streaming tears, wanders bewildered, the Lord of Elephants.†

* *Daritam gata* is obscure. The Scholiast reads दरीं गत:

† This song, which only repeats the former, is probably spurious.

(Mournfully). Alas! ah me! Beholding all quarters of the heavens dark with clouds, and longing for the Mánasa lake, the flamingo has uttered its cry; it was not the tinkling of anklets. *(Having recited this, he rises.)* Well! ere these birds, longing for Mánasa, rise on the wing from this lake, I may find from them some news of my beloved. *(He advances, with Balantiká, and kneels.)* Ho! King of Water-fowl! hereafter shalt thou hie thee to the Mánasa lake; drop thy viaticum of lotus-fibres, to take it presently again; and meanwhile uplift me from my sorrow, by tidings of my beloved; the care of their friends is dearer to the good than even what concerns themselves. *(He looks askance.)* Inasmuch as it lifts its head and looks upward, it tells me plainly, "I have seen her with a longing mind!" *(He sits down, — Charcharí.)* O flamingo! why dost thou hide it? *(He rises and dances.)* If she, my beloved, with the arched brows, hath not passed in the path of thy vision along the shore of the lake, how hast thou stolen all that gait of hers, waving with the intoxication of love? I know it by thy imitation of her walk. *(He advances, with Charchariká, folding his hands.)* O flamingo! give me my fair one; thou hast stolen her gait; she is recognised by that single feature;* thou must surrender what is thus laid to thy charge. *(Again Charcharí.)* Oh! where didst thou learn that sportive step of thine? *(Again Charcharí.*

* Such is the Scholiast's interpretation, *choritadravyánsa.*

He speaks in a courteous tone; then again, with Charcharìká, repeats it in a tone of upbraiding, meditating, with Dwipadiká.) It hath flown away in fear, thinking "It is a King who punishes thieves!" I will seek another opportunity. (*He walks round, with Dwipadiká, and looks.*) Ah! yonder stands a ruddy goose, with its mate. I will walk towards it.

[SONG]

(*Kutiliká.*) In the wood, soul-ravishing with the sounds of the rustlings of the leaves,—(*Mandaghati,*) with the young boughs of its noble trees in full flower,—(*Charcharí,*) the royal elephant wanders, maddened with the absence of his mate.

(*Charcharí, in the interval of two Layas.*) Tell me, O bird of the colour of saffron and the Gorochana dye! hast thou not seen a happy damsel, sporting through these honey days? (*He approaches, with Charchariká, and kneels.*) Oh, bird, named Rathánga! a hero asks thee, deserted by his wife with the swelling hips, and utterly wretched, though possessed of all the pomp that human heart can desire.*— "And who is he?" it asks. I am, then, unknown to it; I, who have as my progenitors the Sun and Moon, whom two brides have chosen of their own accord—Urvas'í and the Empire of the World. What! it still sits silent. Well! I will reprove it. (*He kneels*). Thy own example gives

* I have somewhat expanded these lines, which in the original are obscure as well as very absurd. The continued play on Rathánga marks a later author. For *śronivimba* compare RITU-SANHÁRA, i. 4.

me a precedent. When thy companion is only hidden from thee by the lotus-leaf in the lake, thou fanciest her far away, and longingly utterest a forlorn cry; such, through love of thy mate, is thy fear of being left alone.* What, then, means this aspect towards *me* in my sorrow, refusing all tidings to my heart? (*He sits down.*) This is wholly the effect of my reverses of fortune. Well! I will seek another opportunity. (*Walks on, with Dwipadiká, and looks.*) Ah! this lotus stops me with its bee murmuring within,—like her mouth when I bite her underlip, with a murmur of joyous love. "Show not hostility to the stranger;" thus would I conciliate the bee in its lotus-dwelling.

[SONG]

[*A half Dwichaturasraka.*

The heat of his love on a sudden is greatly increased, and the young swan sports in the lake, entirely surrendered to his passion.

(*He sits down, with a Chaturasraka, folding his hands.*) Oh, honey-making bee! tell me some tidings of her with the wine-like eye; but I know thou hast nowhere seen that peerless wife of mine; for hadst thou found on thy way the perfume that breathes from her lips, what love couldst thou have for this lotus now? (*He walks on, with Dwipadiká, and looks.*) Ah! the King of the Elephant-herd, with his mate, is leaning against yon Kadamba's stem; I will advance towards him.

* Lenz found *bhirutá* in all the MSS.

[SONG]

(*Kutiliká.*) The elephant stands in the wood, mourning for the loss of his mate, with perfume-maddened bees clustering round him!

(*He looks in the interval.*) But this is not the time to approach him. Let him meanwhile seek what his mate offers him with the end of her trunk,—the bough, covered with new shoots, torn from the Śallakí tree, and distilling a juice perfumed like wine. (*Looking, with Sthánaka*). See! he hath finished his repast. Well! I will now draw near and ask him. (*Charcharí.*) I ask thee, O Lord of Elephants! answer me! thou who, with a blow in sport, bendest the stateliest tree! hast thou anywhere seen my mind-enchanting wife, whose beauty far surpasses the Moon? (*He advances two steps.*) Oh, thou young mate of the elephant, mad with love!* and thou, too, O King of the herd! has there passed in the range of your view, a damsel in unfading youth, with a glad aspect—her face like a digit of the Moon, and her hair variegated as the Yúthiká's flowers? (*Joyfully listening.*) Aha! I am consoled by the low sound he utters in his throat, which seems to tell me of the speedy recovery of my beloved. Much do I love thee for our community of rank. Askest thou, "How?" Listen! Me men call the Lord of the Inhabitants of Earth! and thou art the Lord of Elephants; thy bounty flows† in an

* Such is Lenz's and Bopp's version of this obscure phrase.

† Alluding to the juice that flows from the elephant's temples, and which the bees love.

uninterrupted stream, so, too, doth mine; of all fair women, Urvas'í to me is dearest, and of all the herd thy mate to thee; all things of thine are like mine; only mayst thou never feel the anguish of separation! Mayst thou abide in happiness! (*He walks round, with Dwipadiká, and looks.*) Ah! yonder stands the supremely pleasant mountain, Surabhikandhara, beloved of Nymphs,—who knows but my love may be found in the valleys at its foot? (*Walks round and looks.*) What a deep gloom is here! However, I shall see by the flashes of lightning. But stay! through the consequences of my crime, even the rising of the clouds is void of lightning, because of it. Still, I will not depart without visiting this mound of rocks.

[KHANDIKÁ SONG]

See! cleaving the ground with his sharp hoofs, unwavering and overcome with passion, the wild boar rushes round, through the impervious woods, intent on the object of his search.

O mountain with the broad slope! hath my wife with the slender chest and swelling hips, happy as she whom Ananga chose, passed, gracefully bending her head, into thy wood, along the steeps of thy cliffs? How is this? Even it, too, is silent? I fear it cannot hear me through the distance; well! I will go nearer and ask it again.

[CHARCHARÍ SONG]

O thou with thy cataracts clear like the surface

of crystal rocks,—whose peaks are garlanded with a thousand various flowers,—thou who ravishest the heart with the wild songs of thy Kinnaras! O, Supporter of the World! shew me my beloved.

(*He approaches, with Charchariká, and folds his hands.*) Oh, Lord of mountains! hast thou seen in this pleasant extremity of the wood, the lovely damsel peerless in every limb, who is, alas! parted from me? (*He hears the echo; having listened joyfully.*) What! it answers accordingly, "I have seen her." Well! I will look for her. (*Having looked round—as disappointed.*) How is this? It was but my own echo, rolling from the depths of the glens. (*He faints; then having risen and seated himself—in a desponding voice.*) Ah me! I am weary; I will enjoy awhile, on the banks of this mountain torrent, the cool air that blows from its waters. (*He walks round and looks.*) While I gaze on this stream, turbid with the fresh influx of waters, desire rises in my heart. Whence can it come? Frowning with its waves as with brows, girdled with the line of fluttering birds, and throwing off its foam as a garment loosened in anger, and hurrying in devious ways with a repeatedly stumbling step, surely, here is my jealous beloved, changed into the form of the stream! Well! let me conciliate her. Be appeased, O dearest, fairest one! as thou flowest on with thy fluttering and mourning birds, longing for the banks of the Ganges, and resonant with the murmurings of thy swarms of bees.

[CHARCHARÍ SONG]

[*In the interval of a Kutiliká.*

With his arms rising from the surge, lashed by the East Wind, the Lord of Ocean wantonly dances with his limbs of cloud, decked with swans, ruddy geese, and saffron-coloured shells, and encompassed with sea-monsters and dark lotuses; and his open palm is uplifted from the waves near the shore; but the season of new clouds stops him, and draws down the skies against him.*

(*He approaches, with Charcharíká, and kneels.*) O thou with the dear voice! what minutest offence dost thou see in me?—me, whose every desire is bound up in thee, and whose inmost soul revolts from all perjury towards my love,—that thou shouldst thus, in thy haughtiness, fling thy poor servant away? But how? it is still silent. Then is it a river indeed, and no Urvas'í; how else should it thus forsake Pururavas, and hurry onwards to its meeting with the sea? Happiness will be found at last, if we yield not to despair. I will return, then, to that quarter where the fair-eyed damsel vanished from my sight. (*He walks round*

* These lines are the obscurest in the play. In the third line, two of the MSS. collated by Lenz, read *kunkuma* before *s'ankha.* For their sense, he compares a passage in the Nalodáya, where the sea is called अभिगदायादाः, "armed with monsters *(yádáh)*, as with club and sword." Compare the whole in Wilson's translation, and see his note thereon.

and looks.) I will ask yon sitting antelope for tidings of my beloved. (*He kneels*).

[GALITAKA SONG]

In the skirts of the trees, garlanded with new flowers, in the forest of Nandana, soul-ravishing with the sounds of the love-intoxicated Kokilas—consumed with the flame of absence from his mate, roams Airávata, the Lord of Elephants.

(*He looks.*) What is this, that in the form of a black antelope, seems like a side-long glance, let fall by the Beauty of the Grove, to behold the new fruits? His gaze is intently fixed on his doe, which approaches slowly, delayed by the fawn that is drinking her milk. (*Charcharí.*) Hast thou seen a maiden, the beauty of the Suras, full-bosomed, in undecaying youth, with a slender form, a swan's gait, and a deer's eye; wandering through this grove, lighted up by the splendour of the sky? Oh! if thou hast, I beseech thee, deliver me from my sea of desolate sorrow. (*He approaches, folding his hands.*) Ho! Lord of Deer! hast thou seen my beloved in the wood? Listen! I will tell thee her signs; large-eyed, and fair is she to look upon, like thy mate. (*He looks.*) How is this? He minds not my words; his eyes are fixed on his companion. Alas! a reverse of fortune meets with contempt everywhere.* I will pass and seek yet another opportunity. (*He walks round, and looks.*) Aha! I see a sign of her

* *Literally*, "Finds the place of scorn everywhere."

path. Here is a red Kadamba tree, one of whose flowers, uneven with its filaments not yet all expanded* (the herald of the close of the sultry season), has been plucked to adorn my loved one's tresses. (*He walks on, and looks.*) But what is this exceeding glow which I see shining from a fissure in the rock?† Is it not some bright remnant of flesh, from an elephant which some lion hath destroyed? it may be a spark of fire; but could its blaze have endured the rain? Aha! it is a jewel, bright in hue like the blossoms of the red As'oka, and the sun seems resolved to carry it off, with his rays resting on it as hands.‡ Well! I will take it myself.

[SONG]

Withheld from attaining his beloved, his eyes filled with tears, the Lord of Elephants wanders forlorn in the wood, with a countenance wearied with sorrow.

(*He approaches, with Dwipadiká, and seizes it; then says to himself.*)

She, on whose tresses, perfumed with the flowers of the coral tree, this jewel would have been fitly set, —she, my loved one, is now far out of my reach. I will not soil it by my tears.

[*He flings it away.*

* "The Kadamba flower, when full-blown, is invested with projecting antheræ, like the erect bristles of a hedge-hog."—WILSON.

† The King here sees the flash of the distant jewel.

‡ *Kara* means both "a ray," and "a hand."

A VOICE BEHIND THE SCENES.

Seize it, my son—seize it, my son! this is the Jewel of Union, which sprang from the glow of the feet of the daughter of the Mountain;* it bringeth, if it be held fast, speedy union with the beloved.

KING.

[*Looking up.*

Who bids me this? What! it is some holy sage in the form of a deer. O holy sage! I am, indeed, thankful for the counsel. (*He seizes the jewel.*) Welcome, O Jewel of Union! if thou provest the true Jewel of Union to me, forsaken as I am by her of the slender waist,† I will make thee the jewel of my crest, as Is'wara wears the young Moon. (*He walks round and looks.*) But why does this strange feeling of desire come over me; as I gaze on this creeper, bereft of its flowers? yet not without reason is my spirit soothed. This slender plant, with its branches wet with rain, as one whose lips are washed with tears; forlorn of all its adornings, and putting forth no flowers, in the absence of its native season; left alone as in the silence of thought, with no hum of murmuring bees, it stands like my offended love, when she had repelled me in her anger, though fallen suppliant at her feet. I long to embrace the creeper which can give me such an image of her. (*Charcharí.*) Look on me, O creeper! I am agitated

* *Durga*, or *Uma*, the daughter of the Himálaya, and wife of Śiva, or Is'wara.

† For the exact meaning of the epithet, see Lenz, note cx.

of heart;* if ever, by destiny, I may find her again, I will never roam in this forest more; and my wanderings, when this is over, shall never tend hither.

[*He approaches, with Charchariká, and embraces the creeper;* URVAŚÍ *appears in its place.*

KING.

[*Having closed his eyes, and gesticulating as though touched.*

Aha! my heart seems suddenly at rest, as though Urvaśí herself were touched. I may not believe it; how can it be? Whatever have been my first thoughts about Urvaśí, in a moment more they have always proved utterly different. I shall soon open my eyes only to discover that my beloved has not been found to my touch. (*He opens his eyes slowly.*) What? it is Urvaśí herself! [*He faints and falls.*

URVAŚÍ.

Oh, revive! revive! great King!

KING.

[*Coming to himself.*

O dearest! now, indeed, have I life; when thou wast displeased, I was sunk in the gloom of separation from thee: but joy! joy! thou art recovered by me as consciousness by the dead!

* *Vinna-hridaya* is a doubtful word. I have hesitatingly translated it, as the *Prácrit* for *vigna-hridaya*. The Scholiast explains it *viná hridayena*. *Vinna-hridaya* would mean, "I have found my heart," which gives little or no sense in this place. Lenz calls the whole distich, "*absurdum nisi corruptum.*"

URVASÍ.

Let the great King forgive the reverse which my heedless passion brought upon him.

KING.

Thou hast no need to sue my forgiveness; the sight of thee, of itself, hath won it from my inmost soul. Oh, tell me how thou couldst forsake me through such a long weary time. Peacock, Kokila, swan, ruddy goose, bee, elephant, mountain, river, and antelope,—as I roamed in search for thee through the forest, of whom have I not sought tidings with tears?

URVASÍ.

To my inner sense, indeed, were revealed tidings of the King.

KING.

Dearest! I know not what this "inner sense" of thine means.

URVASÍ.

Let the King hear:—in olden time Kartikeya, having taken a vow of eternal celibacy, dwelt in the grove Sakalakalusha, the border of the Gandha-mádana forest, and fixed this decree——

KING.

What?

URVASÍ.

"Whosoever of women shall enter this spot, she shall be changed into the form of a creeper, and she shall not be released from that form, save by the jewel that sprang from the glow of Durgá's feet." I, then—for my heart was blinded by the sage's curse—forgetful of the god's decree, entered the grove of Kumára, to be shunned by all of woman's race, and on the moment of passing within, my form was changed into a creeper, growing by the end of the wood.

KING.

Now, dearest! it is all explained. Thou, who wouldst oft think me banished far away, if thou didst but lose me for a while in sleep,—oh! how couldst thou endure such a long separation as this? See, this, as thou saidst, is the cause of our union—the restorer of the lost.

[*He shews her the jewel.*

URVAŚÍ.

What! strange! it is the Jewel of Union! It is from this that I have regained myself, being once more clasped in the embraces of my King.

KING.

[*Placing the jewel on her forehead.*

Thy face, suffused with the trembling colours of the jewel, which I hold on thy forehead, wears the glow of the lotus, red with the morning sunbeam!

URVAŚÍ.

O speaker of fond words! remember how long we have been absent from Pratishthána; your subjects will begin to blame your tarrying so long; come! let us be going.

KING.

Even so, as you say.

[*They rise to depart.*

URVAŚÍ.

How would the King wish to return?

KING.

Waft me home on the new cloud, converted into a chariot for our happy journey; decorated with the many-coloured bow of Indra, and waving the swift-gleaming lightning for its banner!*

SONG.

Its long-sought companion at last is found; and, every feather erect with joy, the young swan flies on its way,—borne on the air-car of its own wild will.

[*Exeunt.*

* I have borrowed Wilson's translation of this verse, in the Prosody of his Grammar, where I first saw it, several years since. Bopp and Lenz render *khela-gamane,* "in its wavy motion."

END OF THE FOURTH ACT.

ACT V.

Enter the GRACIOSO, *joyfully.*

GRACIOSO.

Aha! aha! heaven be praised! after a long wandering with Urvas'í, in the regions beautiful with the Nandana groves, my Lord the King has at length returned to the city, and now once more exercises his sway, fulfilling the duties of his station, and winning all his subjects' hearts. Well, except the lack of children, I am sure he has not a single subject for sadness. This being a great lunar day, he has been bathing with the Queen, in the meeting waters of the Gangá and Yamuná, and has just returned to the palace; I am here just at the right moment, when he is busy adorning his person with unguents.*

BEHIND THE SCENES.

Hola! hola! a hawk has thrown down the red fan that covered the bright jewel which the King, while parted from the Nymph, had destined for the gem of his diadem, and mistaking the jewel for flesh, has swallowed it and flown off.

GRACIOSO.

[*Listening.*

A most sad mischance! That crest-jewel of re-union I

* The word *vahlabá* is not in the Lexicon. Lenz conjectures that it may be connected with *vahlika*, "saffron."

know was exceedingly prized by my friend. This is why he has risen so hurriedly from his seat, and comes hither with his toilet unfinished. I will attend at his side.

[*Exit.*

END OF THE PRAVEŚAKA.

Enter the KING, GRACIOSO, CHAMBERLAIN, MOUNTAINEER, *and* ATTENDANTS.

KING.

O mountaineer! mountaineer! where is this bird-thief, that has seized its own destruction, and ventures its first theft in the very house of the watchman?

MOUNTAINEER.

Yonder I see it flying about, almost colouring the sky with the jewel, the string of which hangs at the end of its beak.

KING.

I see it now. Bearing the jewel's golden chain suspended from its beak, with its swift flight thus ornamented, the bird makes a ring of its flashing hues, like the circle of a whirling firebrand. But tell me what is to be done.

GRACIOSO.

Away with all feelings of mercy; the offender must be punished.

KING.

You speak well;—a bow! a bow!

ATTENDANTS.

As our Lord commands! [*Exeunt.*

KING.

The vile bird is no longer visible.

GRACIOSO.

There he goes—the wretch has fled away to the south.

KING.

[*Seeing it.*

See now! the bird, with the jewel, that almost buds with splendour, as with a cluster of As'oka blossoms, seems to hang an ear-ring on that quarter of the sky.*

YAVANI SERVANT.

[*Entering with a bow in her hand.*

My Lord! here is the bow with an arrow!

KING.

But what can be done with the bow now? The flesh-eating wretch is flown out of reach of the arrow; yonder gleams the noblest of gems, borne away in the far distance by the bird, as shines the planet Mars by night, half lost in the thick clouds, which he pierces through. Noble Tálavya!

CHAMBERLAIN.

As your Highness commands.

KING.

Command the citizens, by my order; let search be made for the wretched bird in the tree where he roosts at evening.

CHAMBERLAIN.

As the King orders. [*Exit.*

* "Her beauty hangs upon the cheek of night,
Like a rich jewel in an Ethiop's ear."
Romeo and Juliet.

GRACIOSO.

Well! let your Highness rest now; wherever it may be gone, the gem-thief will not escape from the range of your commands. [*They sit down.*

KING.

O my friend! my intense efforts are not for the mere recovery of the gem that the bird has carried off; it is by that jewel of re-union, that I am re-united with my beloved.

CHAMBERLAIN.

[*Entering.*

The King is ever victorious! Transfixed by that wrath of thine which pursued it, the guilty bird, condemned to death, has speedily fallen from the sky with the jewel of the diadem.

[*All express astonishment.*

CHAMBERLAIN.

The jewel has been washed,—to whom should it be given?

KING.

Go, put it in the casket.

MOUNTAINEER.

As the King orders. [*Exit with the jewel.*

KING.

[*To* TÁLAVYA.

Dost thou know whose arrow this is?

CHAMBERLAIN.

It is marked with a name, but my eyes are not equal to the deciphering the colours.

KING.

Hold the arrow up, while I examine it.

GRACIOSO.

What does your Highness study so?

KING.

Hear the letters of the striker's name.

GRACIOSO.

I am all attention.

KING.

[*Reads.*

"This is the arrow of the Prince, the Archer, Áyus, the son of Urvas'í and Pururavas,* the smiter of the lives of his enemies."

GRACIOSO.

Joy! Joy! your Highness is blessed with a son!

KING.

How is this, my friend? Except during the Naimesha sacrifice,† I have been always with Urvas'í; and never have I once seen her giving signs of pregnancy; how then can she have been a mother? Yet I remember, for some days the shade of her face was pale as the Lavali's fruit; and she seemed to wax thin, so that the bracelets round her arms hung loose.‡

GRACIOSO.

Let not your Highness attribute human nature to Urvas'í—the actions of the heavenly beings are veiled by their power.

KING.

Let it be as you say; but what could be the cause of her concealing it?

* *Literally*, "The son of Ilá."

† This lasted twelve years.

‡ Compare *Raghuvans'a*, iii. 2, and Stenzler's note.

GRACIOSO.

Lest you should desert her, as growing old.

KING.

Have done with jesting; think seriously.

GRACIOSO.

Who shall think of the secrets of the gods?

CHAMBERLAIN.

[*Entering.*

May the King be ever victorious! A female ascetic of the race of Bhrigu, has come from the hermitage of Chyavana, bringing a lad with her, and desires to see your Highness.

KING.

Introduce them both without delay.

The CHAMBERLAIN *retires, and re-enters, bringing the* ASCETIC *with the* LAD.

GRACIOSO.

Surely, this is the Kshatriya youth, to whom belonged the arrow inscribed with a name, which pierced the bird as its mark;—in so many ways he takes after your Highness.

KING.

It must be so! My eyes, as they fall on him, are filled with tears; my heart proclaims a father's fondness; and my mind feels a happy calm. How I long to throw off all my gravity of rank and clasp him with a long passionate embrace in my trembling arms! (*Advancing*). Holy woman! I salute thee.

ASCETIC.

O mighty King! long mayst thou be the upholder of the Lunar Race. (*To herself.*) The holy King recognises the ties of blood, even untold. (*Aloud.*) My child! bow to thy father.

[*The* YOUTH, *with his eyes filled with tears,* folds his hands, and bows to the* KING.

KING.

Long mayst thou live, O child!

YOUTH.

[*Starting at being touched,—aside.*

If this be love, which I feel when I hear that this is my father, and I his child; what must, indeed, be their affection for their parents, who have grown up in their bosoms?

KING.

O holy woman! what is the cause of thy coming?

ASCETIC.

Let the great King hear: This child (long may he live) was given into my hands immediately after his birth, for some reason or other, by Urvas'í; all that pertains to the natal rites and education of a well-born Kshatriya was fulfilled towards him by the illustrious Chyavana; and having learned all other knowledge, he hath been lately instructed in archery.

* Or it may be, "The youth bows to the King, whose eyes are filled with tears." This is Lenz's interpretation.

KING.

He has, indeed, become a proficient.

ASCETIC.

This day he went out with some sons of the sages, to collect flowers, fruits, wood, and Kuśa grass; and on his way he violated the prohibitions of the Hermitage.

GRACIOSO.

How so?*

ASCETIC.

A hawk that had carried off some flesh, and was sitting on the summit of one of the trees in the hermitage, became a mark for his arrow.

KING.

And what followed?

ASCETIC.

When the holy man heard the story, he bade me restore my charge into Urvas'í's hands. I desire, therefore, to see Urvas'í.

KING.

Be seated, I pray you. (*They sit down on seats brought by an attendant.*) Oh, honoured Tálavya! inform Urvas'í of this.

[*Exit* CHAMBERLAIN.

KING.

Come hither, come hither, my child; the touch of my son thrills through every limb. Oh! gladden my heart by him brought near me, as the moonbeam gladdens the moon-gem!

* We see Kálidása's light touch in thus making the Gracioso break in upon the conversation by this question of eager curiosity.

ASCETIC.

My child, go and gladden thy father.

[*The youth approaches the* KING.

KING.

(*After embracing him.*)

My child, salute my good friend, the Bráhman!

GRACIOSO.

Why should the child be afraid of me? Surely he must often have seen apes about the hermitage.

YOUTH.

(*Smiling.*)

I salute thee, sir.

GRACIOSO.

May your highness have health and prosper.

[*Enter* URVAŚÍ *and the* CHAMBERLAIN.

CHAMBERLAIN.

This way, your highness,—this way.

URVAŚÍ.

(*Coming forward, aad looking.*)

Who is this sitting on the golden footstool, while the King himself binds up his locks? (*Seeing the* ASCETIC.) Wonderful! it is my boy Áyus, accompanied by Satyavatí; he is grown a tall youth indeed!

KING.

(*Looking.*)

My child, here is thy mother come, intently gazing upon thee,—upheaving the scarf of her bosom, which bursts open with the gush of her love.*

* Compare TENNYSON'S—

"and half
The sacred mother's bosom, panting, burst
The laces towards her babe."

ASCETIC.

Come, my son, go up to thy mother. *(She goes towards* URVAŚÍ *with the youth.)*

URVAŚÍ.

I salute thy feet, O reverend woman!

ASCETIC.

My child, mayst thou ever be honoured of thy husband!

YOUTH.

O honoured one!* I salute thee.

URVAŚÍ.

Win thy father's favour, my child. (*To the* KING.) May the King be ever victorious.

KING.

Hail to the mother! Be seated here.

URVAŚÍ.

Ye honored ones! be seated. (*They all in compliance sit down.*)

ASCETIC.

My child, in the presence of your husband, I now restore into your hands my charge, skilled in knowledge, and exercised in the use of arms and armour. I now wish to depart; I am transgressing the laws of my hermitage-life by a longer stay.

URVAŚÍ.

As you will,—yet seeing you after such an interval, I regret to lose you so soon; but not to violate your laws, perhaps you had better depart;—I trust we shall see each other again.

* Homer's ποτνια.

KING.

Reverend woman! give my salutation to the illustrious Chyavana.

ASCETIC.

Even so.

YOUTH.

Reverend lady! art thou really returning? Wilt thou lead me away too?

KING.

Thou hast performed the duties of thy first order; it is time for thee now to enter the second.

ASCETIC.

My child, follow thy father's words.

YOUTH.

Well, then, send me the dark-necked peacock, whose tail hath lately grown, which used to sleep in my bosom, and loved to feel me stroke its tail.

ASCETIC.

I will do so.

URVAŚÍ.

Holy woman! I salute thy feet.

KING.

I bow to thee, revered one!

ASCETIC.

Happiness unto you all.

[*Exit.*

KING.

Fairest one! this day I am the most fortunate of fathers, with this fair child of thine,—like Indra, the city-destroyer, with Jayanta, the child of his Paulomí.

GRACIOSO.

Well; but why is her highness's face suddenly suffused with tears?

KING.

Why, loveliest one! weepest thou, when joy quivers in my heart at this sudden attainment of continuance to my race, and renderest superfluous the adornings of strings of pearls by the tears that fall fast on thy full bosom?*

URVAŚÍ.

Listen, O King! I was first filled with joy at beholding my child before me; but the mention of Indra's name has recalled to my heart's memory his decree.

KING.

Let it be told.

URVAŚÍ.

Hear, O king!—in the bygone time, when my heart was first made thy prisoner, I was standing one day bewildered with my preceptor's curse, when Indra dismissed me, having fixed a decree.

KING.

What was it? Tell me.

URVAŚÍ.

"When he, my loved friend, the holy King, shall behold the face of a child born from thee, then must thou return unto my presence." Through fear, then, lest I should be parted from thee, to lengthen the time of our union, I entrusted the child into the hands of the honoured Satyavatí, in the

* Lenz found in the MSS. a better reading—*virachanam*.

hermitage of the holy Chyavana; but now that Áyus* has proved himself so worthy to win his father's heart, and has been given unto us again, how can I abide longer with the King? [*The* KING *faints.*

ALL.

Oh! revive, revive, O King!

CHAMBERLAIN.

Revive, O King!

GRACIOSO.

Heaven avert it! Heaven avert it!†

KING.

(Coming to himself.)

Alas, that destiny should delight to check human joy! On me, while I rejoiced in the attainment of my son, hath fallen, O graceful one! this blow of separation from thee, as the lightning falls on the tree, when its languor from the heat is refreshed by the first shower.

GRACIOSO.

This event, I conjecture, will have some foolish accompaniments‡; but King Indra must be conciliated.

URVAŚÍ.

Ah, wretched me! I am undone! The King, I fear, will think that at this moment of my recovery of my son, now

* Dirgháyus is only an auspicious play on Áyus.

† The Scholiast explains *abráhmanyam* by *abadhyoktáviti*. Lenz (*Apparatus Crit.*, p. 31), and Ruckert, consider it "exclamatio hominis perturbati, ut *Germ.* 'Mord!'" Wilson (Lexicon) says," sacred, not to be killed (in theatrical language). E. *a* "not" and *bráhmanya* "proper for a brahmin," *i.e.* death." If so, it may correspond with the French *sacre*. Hofer translates it "O des Unglucks!"

‡ The Gracioso begins to suspect the King's purpose.

that his education is over, I return of my own choice to Swarga, as having accomplished my purpose.

KING.

O loveliest one! speak not thus. The separation is not easy; but our state of dependence on another over-rules our own desires; go, obey thou the commands of thy lord, and I this day devolving my kingdom upon thy son, henceforth will fly for refuge to the woods, where roam the herds of deer.

YOUTH.

Oh, father! put not another under the yoke which the great bull so long hath borne.

KING.

O dear child! say not so; the *Gandha* elephant, though he be young, subdues his fellows; deadly* is the fierce poison of the scarce hatched snake; and the king, though a child, can guard the earth; for the power, that rises equal to every duty, is innate in the blood, not the years. O honoured Tálavya!

CHAMBERLAIN.

Let the King command me.

KING.

Carry my orders to the Minister Parvata;—let the ceremony for anointing King Áyus† be prepared.

[*Exit* CHAMBERLAIN—*sorrowful. All gesticulate as dazzled.*]

* *Prabhavatitarám* is an intensitive form. See *Wilkins' Gram.*, p. 539.

† *A'yushmat* is another auspicious play on *A'yus.*

KING.

(Looking up at the sky.)

Ah! whence is this lightning flash? (*Recognising it.*) Ah! it is the holy Nárada! I see him yonder with his matted locks, tawny like the streak on the touch-stone, and his Bráhmanical thread spotless as a digit of the moon,—a moving Kalpa tree, like a branch of gold, in all the beauty of youth, laden with abundance of pearls. Hasten with the oblation to honour him!

URVAŚÍ.

Behold the oblation for the holy sage.

NÁRADA.

(*Entering.*)

Victory to the Guardian of the Middle World.

KING.

O holy sage! I salute thee.

URVAŚÍ.

I bow before thee!

NÁRADA.

May husband and wife be never parted!

KING.

(*Aside to* URVAŚÍ.)

Would that it might be so. (*Aloud.*) My child, born of Urvaśí, bows to thee.

NÁRADA.

Long live the youth.

KING.

Be seated on this seat. [*They all sit down.*

KING.

(*Respectfully.*)

What may be the cause of thy coming?

NÁRADA.

O King! hear the commands of Indra.

KING.

I attend.

NÁRADA.

Indra, who beholds all things by his divine power commands thee, who art purposing to depart into the wood....

KING.

What commands he?

NÁRADA.

It hath been foretold by those who behold the three worlds, that ere long there will be war between the Suras and Asuras, and thou must be our ally in the fight; lay not, therefore, thy weapons aside, and Urvaśí shall be thy rightful wife while life shall last.

URVAŚÍ.

O wonderful! an arrow seems plucked from my heart!

KING.

Immeasurable are my obligations to the supreme King.

NÁRADA.

It is well! let him fulfil his duties towards thee, and do thou fulfil thine towards him; with their several splendours the sun augmenteth fire, and fire the sun. (*Looking up to the sky.*) O Rambhá! let the consecrated water be brought for the youth's coronation.

RAMBHÁ.

[*Entering.*

All the preparations are ready.

NÁRADA.

Let the youth be seated on the royal seat.*

* *Literally*, "Seat of prosperity."

RAMBHÁ *places him on the royal seat.*

NÁRADA.

Hail! hail!

KING.

Mayst thou be the exalter of thy race!

URVASÍ.

May thy father's words come true!

[*A pair of* BARDS *behind the Scene*].

FIRST BARD.

As Atri, the sage of the Immortals, to Bráhma, the creator; as the Moon to Atri; as Budha to the Moon; as our King to Budha;—so thou, O Prince! art like to thy father, in all world-loved qualities; and all blessings are fulfilled in thy prëeminent race.

SECOND BARD.

Erst firmly fixed in thy father, and now entrusted to thee in thy turn, whose stable might knoweth no sickness to impair it,—the Royal Prosperity shineth yet brighter than ever; like Gangá, who rolleth her waters at once in the Himálaya and the ocean.

RAMBHÁ.

Joy! joy! my loved friend beholds her son's coronation. and yet needs not to be parted from her husband.

URVASÍ.

Our happiness, Rambhá, is common to us both. (*Taking the* YOUTH *by the hand.*) My child! salute thy elder mother.

KING.

Stay! let us all approach her together.

NÁRADA.

The glory of thy son Áyus' coronation recals to my mind the day when Indra appointed Mahásena to the command of his hosts.

KING.

Greatly, indeed, am I favoured by Indra.

NÁRADA.

Say, O King! what further boon wouldst thou have the Lord of fulness bestow on thee?

KING.

If there be any further boon that is dear to me, then let Indra grant, that, through thee, for the common welfare of the good,* the mutual rivals Fortune and Eloquence may at last be wedded in that union which now seems so hard to be attained. And yet another still: May every one pass safely through his straits! may every one behold good fortune! may every one attain his desires! and every one be everywhere happy!

* All the MSS. collated by Lenz read, *udbhútaye.*

THE END.

A SCHEME

OF THE

METRES OCCURRING IN THE VIKRAMORVAŚÍ.*

I HAVE not thought it necessary to specify the instances of the Epic s'loka, which are pretty frequent (twenty-seven in all); the other metres are as follows :—

I.—DISTICHS WHICH CONSIST OF FOUR EQUAL *PA'DAS.*

a. TRISHTUBH, or distichs of forty-four syllables:

1. *Indravajrá* pure.

— — ⏑ — — ⏑ ⏑ — ⏑ — —

p. 54 (6).

2. *Upajáti;* or *Indravajrá* and *Upendravajrá* mixed.

⏓ — ⏑ — — ⏑ ⏑ — ⏑ — —

p. 8, ii. iii.; 59, i.; 60, ii.

* This analysis only extends to the *Sanskrit* part of Act IV. The Prákrit metres are of a different class; and as the Prákrit passages appear in Mr. Williams' edition in their Sanskrit form only, no notice of them is needed here. The numbers here given refer to the page and the number of the distich in that page,—except in the Fourth Act, (pages 38 to 57), where the second numbers refer to the *line* in the page.

b. JAGATÍ, or distichs of forty-eight syllables :

3. *Vanśashtha.*

⏑—⏑ ——⏑ ⏑—⏑ —⏑—

p. 2, ii.; 4, ii.; 32, i. ii.; 43 (8); 54 (17); 55 (14).

4. *Drutavilambita.*

⏑⏑⏑ —⏑⏑ —⏑⏑ —⏑—

p. 14, i.; 28, i; 50 (21); 52 (9).

c. ATIJAGATI, or distichs of fifty-two syllables :

5. *Manjubháshiní.*

⏑⏑— ⏑—⏑ ⏑⏑— ⏑—⏑ —

p. 53 (9); 57 (11).

d. ŚAKKARÍ, or distichs of fifty-six syllables :

6. *Vasantatilaka.*

——⏑ —⏑⏑ ⏑—⏑ ⏑—⏑ ——

p. 2 (Intro.); 18, i.; 19, i.; 36, ii.; 37, i.; 43 (2); 45 (5); 46 (22); 61, ii.; 65, i.; 66, i.; 67, i.

e. ATIŚAKKARÍ, or distichs of sixty syllables :

7. *Máliní.*

⏑⏑⏑ ⏑⏑⏑ ——— ⏑—— ⏑——

p. 13, i*; 44 (10); 45 (19); 49 (3); 66, ii.; 68. ii. iii.

f. ATYASHTÍ, or distichs of sixty-eight syllables :

8. *Mandákrántá.*

——— —⏑⏑ ⏑⏑⏑ ——⏑ ——⏑ ——

p. 3: iii; 10. i.; 26, i.; 42 (11).

* In the third line read "ápán'd'u."

9. *Hariní.*

⌣⌣⌣ ⌣⌣— ——— —⌣— ⌣⌣— ⌣—

p. 16, i.; 30. i.; 41 (2); 48 (14); 66, iii.

10. *Prithwí.*

⌣—⌣ ⌣⌣— ⌣—⌣ ⌣⌣— ⌣—— ⌣—

p. 16, ii.

11. *Sikhariní.*

⌣—— ——— ⌣⌣⌣ ⌣⌣— —⌣⌣ ⌣—

p. 51 (17); 53 (21).

g. Atidhrití, or distichs of seventy-six syllables:

12. *S'árdúla víkríd'ita.*

——— ⌣⌣— ⌣—⌣ ⌣⌣— ——⌣ ——⌣ —

p. 1 (Bened.); 2, i; 4, i; 13, ii.; 22, i.; 24, i.; 26, ii.; 34, ii.; 41 (10)*; 50 (5); 54 (24).

II.—DISTICHS OF TWO EQUAL *ARDHA*-ŚLOKAS, WITH UNEQUAL *PÁDAS.*

13. *Aupachchhandasika.*

⌣⌣— ⌣⌣— ⌣—⌣ —— | ⌣⌣— —⌣⌣ —⌣— ⌣——

p. 6, iv.; 8, i.; 19, iii.; 28, ii.; 41 (17); 47 (6).

14. *Aparavaktrá.*

⌣⌣⌣⌣⌣⌣—⌣—⌣— | ⌣⌣⌣⌣—⌣⌣—⌣—⌣—

p. 23, ii.

15. *Pushpitágrá.*

⌣⌣⌣⌣⌣⌣—⌣—⌣—— | ⌣⌣⌣⌣—⌣⌣—⌣—⌣——

p. 27, i.; 37, iii.

16. *Vaitálíya.*

⌣⌣—⌣⌣—⌣—⌣— | ⌣⌣——⌣⌣—⌣—⌣—

p. 45 (12).

* The *athavá* in the tenth line should be struck out, as it mars the metre.

III.—DISTICHS, WHOSE FEET ARE RECKONED BY SYLLABIC INSTANTS.

17. ***A'ryá.*** (For this measure see the ***Hitopades'a***).

p. 3, i. ii.; 4, iii.; 5, i.; 11, i.; 12, i.; 13, iii.; 23, i.; 27, ii. iii.; 29, i.; 34, i.; 35, i. ii.: 42 (24)*; 43 (16); 49 (15, 25); 53 (17); 54 (12)†; 56 (21); 57 (4); 59, iii.; 60, i.; 61, i,; 62, i.; 63, i.; 64, i.

18. ***A'ryá Upagítí*** (differing from the preceding in the second ***páda,*** which, like the fourth, contains only fifteen short syllables).

p. 1, ii. (Intro.)

The verses, page 52 (19), are very irregular. (*See* Lenz, p. 213).

* In line 25, the metre requires ***smărayati.***

† In line 13 the metre requires ***priyă-janena.***